I Love VEGETARIAN

Fast and easy recipes containing common ingredients
found in local supermarkets and health food stores.
Whether losing or maintaining weight, improving health,
or reducing or eliminating animal products, the recipes are
great for people of all ages, health conditions, and lifestyles.

Sheri Fisher, Ph.D.

A New Hope for Health

Published by
A New Hope for Health
www.anewhopeforhealth.com

Photography
M. Darling Photography
Melissa Darling
www.mdarlingphotography.com
435-229-3338

Design and layout
Dimension Design & Print, Inc.
St. George, Utah
www.ddap.net

International Standard Book Number (ISBN): 0-9726037-1-9

Printed in the United States of America
2nd Printing

Order copies from:

A New Hope for Health

website: www.anewhopeforhealth.com

email: anewhopeforhealth@infowest.com

CONTENTS

Dedication

To my family, with love. And, to all those who want a more happy, healthy, and gentle lifestyle.

Acknowledgements

Many people have been instrumental in the development of this cookbook. A special thanks to my son, Cameron Payne - a gourmet and healthy chef. He graduated from Northwest Culinary Arts School in Portland, Oregon. He is currently the Executive Chef for "The Biggest Loser at Fitness Ridge" in Southern Utah where he focuses on a low-fat, healthy cuisine. He has shared many recipes, ideas, creativity in food presentation for the pictures and time in helping me complete this cookbook.

Thanks goes to all my family who, for years, were the "guinea pigs" for my many trial and error recipes and helped me label them as "keepers" or "throw aways". They are appreciated for their patience as changes in their dietary habits often came without warning or consent. Especially to my sons, Cameron and Royce, who grew up eating out of our family garden and easily learned to love a variety of foods. Cooking was exciting and fun because of their willingness to try so many new things. A special thanks to my younger son, Royce, also in the culinary field, who has also shared his knowledge and expertise now in a management position in restaurant industry.

I greatly appreciate my husband, Brian, for his support and encouragement. He spent countless hours assisting me with the computer and technical aspect involved in publishing this cookbook. Along with his son David, I add a big "thanks" for their good sense of humor and open mind while I struggled, at times, in experimenting and testing recipes.

Thanks to Melissa Darling of M. Darling Photography. Without her creative genius the cookbook would not have been as delightful!

Introduction

I have learned one very important thing over the years. If I see a restaurant that advertises: "Country Style", "Mom's", "Home Cooking", "Family Dining", or the like, I turn and run – while I still can! Once I began focusing on a healthy, low saturated fat diet, I also began seeking out good, healthy restaurants.

Generally, the type of food served at those establishments are high in fat, high in refined products such as white flour and sugar, and low in fiber. A steady diet of this type of food can lead to a variety of common health problems such as high blood pressure, high cholesterol, heart disease, obesity, diabetes, and cancer.

A serious problem in our Standard American Diet (S.A.D.) is that a typical meal resembles the type of restaurants listed above. To make matters even worse, we add more processed foods, loaded with colors, additives, preservatives, and "scary" chemicals.

While lecturing at various health and fitness centers and I encourage people to eat healthy by getting back to food basics, reducing or eliminating animal products, and avoiding refined and processed foods. Most of us feel we do not have the time to spend on preparing healthy meals. Sometimes it's difficult finding healthy, less common, ingredients. Many of us are afraid to change our eating habits and try new things for fear that "*my* family would never eat that way."

Therefore, I have come up with fast, easy recipes that contain common ingredients found in local supermarkets and health food stores. Whether losing weight, improving health, or reducing or eliminating animal products, the recipes are great for people of all ages, health conditions, and lifestyles.

The recipes are vegetarian (no meat, fish or poultry). Vegan (no animal products of any kind) substitutions are found in the substitution list and in many recipes. Substitutions are so much easier to use and have such a great taste these days. We can now find sour cream, cream cheese, cheeses, yogurt, and other traditional dairy products made with soy, grains, nuts, and seeds. They are generally lower in fat and do not contain cholesterol. Using the vegan version of a recipe will lower the fat content, and vary the taste and texture somewhat.

By practicing a more vegetarian / vegan lifestyle, using the recipes found in this book, and incorporating the listed substitutions into your own recipes, you will enjoy a healthier life. As you try these recipes, you will find that vegetarian / vegan food is flavorful, colorful, and satisfying. You will probably not even miss the "meat".

Each recipe lists the nutritional analysis for those wishing to keep track of their calorie, fat, carbohydrate, fiber, and/or protein intake. On a vegetarian/vegan diet, you can consume a little more fat than on the S.A.D. because the type of fat is healthier and less likely to add on extra weight. Animal products contain cholesterol and saturated fat. The recipes in this cookbook contain mostly plant fats which are rarely saturated or contain cholesterol.

Eating should be fun, satisfying, and enjoyable. We are made to eat - not to diet and deprive ourselves of nutrients physically, mentally, or emotionally. If you eat a variety of healthy foods, as shown throughout this cookbook, you will not need to obsess about the amount of fat and calories consumed. I recommend just eating healthy, in moderation – and enjoy!

Substitution List

Alcohol –

   a. white wine – white grape juice, apple cider, apple juice, vegetable stock, water

   b. sake – chickenless broth, 1 c. water + 1 T. diluted rice vinegar

   c. vodka – water, apple cider or white grape juice mixed with lime juice

   d. sherry – apple cider, white grape juice + vanilla extract

   e. rum – white grape juice + vanilla or rum extract

   f. red wine – 1 c. water + 2 T. balsamic vinegar, grape juice, vegetable stock, cranberry juice

   g. amaretto – white grape juice + almond extract, marzipan

   h. Champagne or other sparkling wines – sparkling apple cider, sparkling cranberry juice, or sparkling grape juice.

Baking powder – 1 tsp. Baking powder = 1 t. baking soda + 1 t. cream of tartar.

Butter – for baking purposes, Spectrum brand has an all vegetable shortening made from palm oil. It contains no hydrogenated oil or trans fats. For a spread, use olive or flax seed oil. If you want to use some butter, soften butter to room temperature and add equal amounts of olive or flaxseed oil and whip until smooth. Chill to harden. This way you only get one half the amount of butter. Another brand of margarine without the trans fats is Earth Balance.

Chocolate – carob (comes in powder or solid form)

Cornstarch – per 1 T. cornstarch: use 2 t. arrowroot powder or kudzu (kuzu), or 2 T. flour, or 1 T. granular tapioca. Use pureed fruit or vegetables.

Dairy –

Milk: use equal amounts of rice, soy, or nut milks. If the recipe calls for sour or buttermilk, add 1 T. apple cider vinegar or 2 tsp. lemon juice to 1 c. milk substitute. There are ice cream substitutes such as frozen Rice Dream.

Cheese: use soy, rice, or almond cheese, sour cream, and cream cheese (Toffutti is a great brand for a sour cream and cream cheese substitute). Crumbled tofu can be used in a recipe to replace cottage or ricotta cheese.

Eggs - per 1 egg (for extra leavening you can add 1 t. baking soda)

   a. Energee Egg Replacer – a potato starch used for baking. See instructions.
   b. Pureed flaxseeds – 1 c. flax seeds + 2 c. water (blend seeds to a powder add water and blend until smooth. ¼ cup = 1 egg)   Keep refrigerated
   c. Pureed tofu – 2 oz – mix with enough water to make about the consistency of an egg.
   d. 1 t. unflavored gelatin (Emes brand) + 3 T. cold water plus 2 T. gelatin + 1 t. boiling water.
   e. Pureed banana – 2 oz

Gelatin – regular gelatin such as Jello contains animal products. The Emes brand gelatin is plant based. Agar-agar is a sea vegetable made into powder or flakes. 1 T. gelatin = 2 T. agar flakes.

Grains – many recipes call for whole grains – usually wheat or rice. For fun and healthy varieties or because of allergies try experimenting with other whole grains such as : kamut, spelt, rye, barley, brown rice, buckwheat, cous cous, quinoa, corn, oats, and millet.

Mayonnaise – to use a vegan product Hain's or Veganaise has an eggless mayonnaise or you can make your own using the tofu mayonnaise recipe

Meat - tempeh (a cultured soy food mixed with various grains), seitan (made from wheat gluten), beans, tofu (an easily digestible soy bean curd), soy cheese, textured vegetable protein (TVP). Boca, Melissa's, Amy's, and Lite Life are great brands.

Nuts – to lower the fat content of a recipe replace the nuts with Post Grape-Nuts cereal. They make a great low-fat replacement for a graham cracker crust. Just pour equal amount in the bottom of a pie plate. Slowly and carefully spoon your filling over the top so as not to move the cereal.

Oil –

Baking: use 1 – 2 cups applesauce per 1 cup of oil or use equal amount of pureed banana. Or you can use an equal amount of arrowroot mixture (see instruction below)

Salad dressings: use 1 c. arrowroot powder, 1 c. cold water + 1/2 gal. water. Blend the 1 c. powder with the 1 c. water to dissolve. Place the 1/2 gal. water in a pan and bring to boil stirring constantly. Slowly add the mixture stirring constantly. Chill before using.

Sautéing – use water, apple juice, vegetable or other broth.

Soy Sauce – Bragg's Liquid Aminos and tamari sauce. Bragg's contains amino acids and is generally lower in salt. Tamari sauce is a soy sauce that contains no sugar and is available "wheat free."

Stock – Frontier brand has a vegetable, meatless chicken, and meatless beef broth powders. Imagine brand also puts out various broths already in liquid form. Use miso (fermented soy bean paste) diluted with water.

Sugar – per 1 cup substitution

Sweetener	Amount	Reduce Liquid
barley/rice syrup	1 c	---
honey	1 c	1/8 c
fruit juice	2/3-3/4 c.	1/8 c
maple syrup	1 c	1/8 c
molasses	1 c	---
stevia	1 t.	* add 1/8 c
fructose	1 c	--

Vinegar – cranberry juice, lemon or lime juice, vitamin C powder (ascorbic acid).

Wheat – If you have sensitivity to wheat, try replacing 50% to 100 % of the recipe with other flours such as: Kamut, spelt, rice, oat, rye, barley, buckwheat, etc.

Pantry List

Below are some products that are a great addition to any pantry. Some brands and products that have been shown to perform successfully and taste great are listed below. Experiment with other brands.

1. **Rice, soy, almond milks** – Imagine brand makes milk substitutes called Rice Dream and Soy Dream. There are many others on the market such as Pacific or Silk. The tastes vary somewhat.

2. **Tofu** –is a white curd made from soybeans and a coagulant. The Japanese style packaged in aseptic packages such as the Mori Nu brand is great for salad dressings, puddings, smoothies, etc. The Chinese style is packaged in water. It is even more nutritious and is great for stir-fries, casseroles, marinating, grilling, etc.

3. **Bragg's Liquid Aminos** – this sauce can be used in place of any soy sauce and contains amino acids. Spray on vegetables or use as a soy sauce or marinade.

4. **Nut Butters: Sesame Tahini, peanut, or almond** – a sesame nut butter used in many different types of cooking. Use nut butters in salad dressings, sandwiches, baked items, or dips.

5. **Fructose** – can be used in place of sugar. It is much sweeter than sugar so use less (see substitution list). It is a lower glycemic sweetener and contains about 1/3 the calories of sugar.

6. **Emes gelatin or Agar Agar** – Emes is a plant based gelatin that can be used in place of regular gelatin. Also, **agar-agar** can be used the same way and is made from a sea algae.

7. **Baby foods** – buy baby apple juice, white grape juice, apple sauce, etc. They come in just the right amounts for cooking so there is no waste. They are usually juice without the added sugar.

8. **Broths or Stocks** - Frontier brand provides broth powders that are meatless such as vegetable, chickenless, meatless, and cream of chickenless. They store for a long time and are easy to use. They do not contain MSG or other harsh chemicals or additives. Some broths come prepared and are also vegetarian such as Imagine or Westbrae companies. Check your health food store for other brands.

9. **Carob** – is made from a ground pod off of the tamarind tree. Use it in place of chocolate. Keep on hand carob powder, and carob chips for cooking or beverages. It is high in calcium and does not contain caffeine. People allergic to chocolate can usually tolerate carob.

10. **Various grains** - keep on hand different grains for recipes calling for whole grains. It gives variety to the dishes and each contains their own specific nutrients. Use grains such as kamut, spelt, rye, barley, brown rice, buckwheat, cous cous, quinoa, amaranth, corn, millet, and oats.

11. **Energee Egg Replacer** – a great egg substitute in powdered form that can be used in baking. It is made out of potato starch. Look for other egg replacers in your local health food store.

12. **Spectrum shortening** – use in recipes calling for butter, shortening or margarine. It is made from palm oil and does not contain trans fats or hydrogenated oil.

13. **Post Grape Nuts** – can be used in place of nuts in most recipes and also as a substitute for a graham cracker crust.

14. **Beans** - keep a variety of canned and dried beans on hand. The canned beans can be used when in a hurry. Buy seasoned and unseasoned varieties. Try kidney, black, pinto. Garbanzo (chickpeas), and white.

15. **Herbs** - keep both dry and fresh on hand. If you have the space, grow your own in pots or in the ground. Fresh herbs are healthy, and contain essential oils. They taste great in salads or soups.

16. **Baking powder** – buy brands that are aluminum free such as Rumford, Bob Mills, and Red Star.

17. **Vinegars** – apple cider vinegar is healthier than white distilled. Also keep on hand rice and seasoned vinegars.

18. **Oils** – use only cold or expeller pressed oils and keep them refrigerated. Use oils such as olive, flax, sunflower, peanut, or sesame.

19. **Flaxseeds** – flaxseeds are great to add to recipes-whole or ground. They add extra fiber and essential fatty acids. Grind them for the "egg replacer" recipe, to use in baked items, or sprinkle over you favorite cereal, or salad. Add them to "smoothies".

20. **Arrowroot powder** – is a healthier alternative to cornstarch. It is a tropical starchy herb and less refined.

21. **Kuzu (Kudzu) root** - is another substitute for cornstarch. Kuzu is a high alkalizing sea vegetable root.

22. **Sea Vegetables** – these include: Agar Agar, Dulse, Hijiki, Kelp, Kombu, Kuzu, Nori, Wakame and others that you can find at your local health food store. They are loaded with minerals and vitamins. Add them to salads, salad dressings, soups, casseroles, or any other recipe you wish.

23. **Blackstrap molasses** - is rich in minerals, especially iron and calcium. Use as a flavoring agent or as a daily supplement.

24. **Sea or Mineral salt** – these salts have kept all of their minerals during processing. They are not loaded with harmful chemicals.

25. **Mayonnaise** – look for "eggless", it is lower in fat and cholesterol. Hain's or Veganaise brand, along with others in local health food stores.

Spice Up Your Life

VEGGIES	SPICES
Artichokes	parsley
Beans	cumin, mint, thyme, basil
Beets	caraway, dill
Broccoli	mace, nutmeg
Brussel Sprouts	mace, nutmeg
Cabbage	caraway, fennel
Carrots	caraway, cinnamon, clove, dill
Cauliflower	curry, mace, nutmeg, savory, fennel
Corn	mint, cumin, parsley
Cucumbers	dill, mint
Eggplant	oregano, sage, thyme, basil
Green beans	dill
Lentils	curry, savory, cumin, basil
Lima beans	curry, savory, cumin, basil
Mushrooms	oregano, rosemary, tarragon, thyme
Onions	nutmeg, savory
Peas	chervil, mint
Peppers	oregano, marjoram, cilantro
Potatoes	caraway, curry, dill, mint, rosemary, thyme, basil
Rice	coriander/cilantro, curry, dill, ginger, turmeric
Spinach	nutmeg
Summer squash	oregano, thyme, basil
Sweet potatoes	allspice, cardamom, cinnamon, clove
Tomatoes	basil, dill, cilantro, oregano, savory, tarragon, thyme
Turnips	caraway
Winter squash	allspice, caraway, clove, cardamom, cinnamon
Zucchini	parsley, basil

HERBS	FOODS
Basil	tomato dishes, salads, pasta dishes, sauces, stews
Bay leaf	soups, beans, stews, stuffing, salad dressings, spiced vinegar
Borage	salads, beverages
Caraway seed	rye bread, Cole slaw, soups, salads
Cardamon seed	cinnamon bread, coffee cake, fruit salads
Cayenne (red pepper)	Mexican food, pickles, stews, beans, pasta dishes
Cinnamon	desserts, apples, beets, squash, pumpkin, sweet potatoes, rice, cider
Cloves	sauces, gravies, pastries, desserts, fruit juices
Coriander seed	breads, soups, sauces, stews, gravies
Cumin seed	Mexican food, Middle Eastern food, curry, beans
Dill seed	salads, salad dressings, potato soup, vinegar, pickles
Fennel seed	breads, pickles, soups, sauerkraut, desserts
Garlic	beans, ethnic foods, vegetables, salad dressings
Ginger	vegetables, fruits, Chinese food
Lemon grass	sauces, pickles, oriental tea
Marigold	fresh or dried flowers in soups, salads, desserts
Marjoram	used like or with basil, sage, oregano, etc.
Mint	jellies, beverages (esp. teas), fruit salads, Tabouleh, sauces
Nutmeg	potatoes, desserts, custards, rice, carrots, sweet potatoes, cauliflower
Oregano	Mexican and Italian food, soups, salad dressings, stews
Paprika	Hungarian dishes, hummus, potatoes salads, cheese dishes,

Parsley	eggs, beans, soups, salads, salad dressings, garnish
Rosemary	gravies, sauces, rice, salads, salad dressings,
Saffron	cakes, breads, desserts, rice, eggs, sauces
Sage	soups, salads, vegetables
Savory	beans, peas, lentils, vegetables
Sesame seed	breads, granola, casseroles, Chinese food, salad dressings, soups
Tarragon	French food, gravies, tartar sauce, soups, pickles
Thyme	French food, rice, salad dressings, soups, salads,
Turmeric	mustard, mayonnaise, salads (egg or "eggless"), curried dishes
Vanilla	desserts, breads

Sprouting

Sprouts are one of the healthiest foods we have on our planet. It is important that we spend a little time understanding the importance of sprouting, what to sprout and how to go about it. Seeds are the foundation of living foods. While they are dry they can store for years. This makes them valuable to have on hand in times of emergency, illness, financial struggles, or healthier eating.

Importance of Sprouting

Sprouting activates enzymes in the seeds that are vital to good health. Proteins, carbohydrates, and starches are made easier for the body to digest and assimilate. Vitamin and mineral contents are increased, and when sprouts are allowed to turn green, become rich in chlorophyll.

Sprouts are easy to grow and cheap to produce. The seeds can store for a long time and a variety of sprouts can be enjoyed throughout the year. Sprouts are also very cooling and cleansing to the body. They are full of energy and therefore we increase our own energy when we consume them.

Sprouting increases the nutrient content and helps the digestive process. It also reduces the cooking time.

What to Sprout

All beans/legumes such as mung, garbanzos, pintos, or adzuki can be sprouted. Seeds such as alfalfa, clover, radish, broccoli, pumpkin, sunflower, or mustard make great sprouts. Because nuts are hard for many people to digest, sprouting almonds, cashes, cashew, pecans and walnuts will help digestion along. You can also sprout grains such as wheat, buckwheat, kamut, brown rice, and millet.

How to Sprout

1. Soak seeds overnight (no more than 12 hours).
2. Place seeds in a large jar covered with cheesecloth or use a sprouter.
3. If using a jar lay the jar on its side at a 45-degree angle so it can drain.   Be sure air can circulate in the jar.
4. Rinse seeds 3 or 4 times a day using purified water.
5. Sprouts usually take about 3-6 days.
6. Store sprouts in refrigerator and rinse daily.

* There are many books available on sprouting. Seeds packages will also have directions on the amount to use and the length of time to harvest.

Southwest Potato Skins

Fruit Smoothie

Categories   Appetizers / Beverages

You can mix and match any of your favorite fruits and juices.
Serve as a breakfast drink or at snack time. You can add protein
or green drink powder for a great protein or energy drink. Add
fresh greens such as kale, collard greens, Swiss chard, or
sprouts for an extra boost of important nutrients.

Serves 1   Yields 2 cups Preparation   Time 10 minutes

1 c	pineapple juice, (orange, apple, cranberry, carrot)
1/8 c	tofu
1/2 med	banana
4-5	strawberries, fresh or frozen fruit (mangos, peaches, etc)
1 t	nutritional yeast
1 t	flax seed

Blend in blender until smooth. May also add ice and blend until
thick.

Per Serving: approx. 150 Calories; 3g Fat; 6g Protein;
56g Carbohydrate; 5g Dietary Fiber

Green Onion Dip

Categories   Appetizers / Beverages

This dip is great for chips, vegetables, or a topping for potatoes.
To serve, pour into bell pepper shells or serving dishes. You may
also add to or replace the green onions with 2/3 c. spinach-
frozen and thawed, 1/4 c diced olives or bell peppers.

Serves   12   Yields 2 cups   Preparation Time 15 minutes

1 c	tofu sour cream or plain soy yogurt
1 c	mayo (Veganaise, etc.)
1/4 c	chopped green onions
1/4 c	chopped fresh parsley
1-2	garlic cloves

Blend sour cream, mayo, green onions and parsley until smooth.
Add minced garlic and pulse until blended. Chill to blend
flavors.

Per Serving: 70 Calories; 7g Fat; 2g Protein;
2g Carbohydrate; trace Dietary Fiber

Hummus

Categories   Appetizers / Beverages

Hummus is a Middle Eastern dish. It is full of protein and calcium. A great appetizer by spreading on pitas or tortillas, for dipping vegetables, or as a sandwich spread. *See Hummus and Veggie Rollups recipe.

Serves 12   Yields about 16 oz   Preparation Time 10 minutes

2 c	garbanzo beans
3 med	garlic clove
3 T	tahini (see pantry list)
1/4 c	lemon juice
1/2 t	cumin
1/2 t	paprika
1/2 t	salt

Blend all in a blender until smooth. Chill to blend seasonings. Garnish with fresh parsley.

Per Serving: 147 Calories; 4g Fat; 7g Protein; 22g Carbohydrate; 6g Dietary Fiber

Meatless Balls

Categories   Appetizers / Beverages

*This dish is listed in the appetizer section because they can be
served as hors d'oeuvres. They are also great in a pasta sauce,
BBQ sauce, brown gravy, sweet and sour sauce, creamed soup,
or plain as a side or main dish. Form into patties for great
veggie burgers.*

Serves 8   Yields about 24 balls   Preparation Time 15 min

1 16-oz pkg	tofu block, Chinese style, drained, press out moisture
1/3 c	walnuts, diced fine
1/3 c	bread crumbs
1/4 c	wheat flour
1/2 t	salt
1 T	parsley
1/2 t	oregano
1/2 t	basil
1/2 c	onion, minced
1 T	Bragg's amino liquids (see pantry list), or soy sauce.

In a large bowl, mash tofu. Add the rest of the ingredients and
with your hands, mix well. Form into 1-2 balls. (You can pulse
in a blender or food chopper to combine). Lightly spray a baking
sheet and bake at 375 until brown about 20-30 minutes.

If using in a pasta sauce, after baking, place in the sauce and
bake for 30 minutes more and pour over noodles.

*Per Serving: 103 Calories; 5g Fat; 7g Protein;
157g Carbohydrate; 1g Dietary Fiber*

Party Cheese Ball

Categories   Appetizers / Beverages

This cheese ball is great for entertaining and special occasions.
Serve with crackers, fresh vegetables or chips. For a variation,
you may also add diced black olives or a little garlic powder.

Serves   16   Yields 4 1/2 cups   Preparation Time 20 minutes

2 8-oz pkg	soy cream cheese, room temperature
1 c	pineapple, crushed and drained
1/4 c	bell pepper, diced
2 T	green onion, diced
1 c	almond, sliced
1 t	salt

Combine ingredients except for nuts and roll into one large or
two small balls. Roll in sliced almonds to coat. Chill until firm
(4-6 hours)

Per Serving: 139 Calories; 13g Fat; 3g Protein;
4g Carbohydrate; 1g Dietary Fiber

Southwest Potato Skins

Categories   Appetizers / Beverages

Not only is this a great appetizer, but also a great main or side dish! Bake potatoes ahead of time and keep in refrigerator until ready to use. Use leftover potatoes for soups, burritos, hash browns, mashed potatoes, etc.

Serves 8   Yields 16 halves   Preparation Time 15 minutes
                                   (if potatoes are pre-baked)

8 lg	potatoes, baked and halved
6 oz	soy cheese, grated
1/2 c	tomatoes, diced
1/2 c	olives, diced
1/4 c	green onion, diced
1/2 c	salsa
1/2 c	soy sour cream
	garnish with guacamole dip (optional)

Preheat oven to 400. Scoop out 1/2 potato out of each half. Fill with all of the above except guacamole, salsa, and sour cream. Place in oven and bake until cheese is melted (5-8- minutes). Garnish with guacamole, salsa, and sour cream.

Per Serving: 228 Calories; 4g Fat; 8g Protein; 48g Carbohydrate; 5g Dietary Fiber

Tofu Power Smoothie

Categories   Appetizers / Beverages

High in protein, fiber, and calcium, this drink is a great way to start the day. Use as a protein drink before or after exercise.

Serves   3   Yields 4 1/2 cups   Preparation Time 10 minutes

1/2 c	tofu, lite silken
1 c	soy or rice milk
1 1/2 c	apricot nectar, (peach, strawberry, etc)
1 c	pineapple juice, (orange, apple, etc)
1 T	nutritional yeast
1 t	flax seed
1/2 c	alfalfa sprouts, or other fresh greens such as parsley, carrot or beet tops, spinach, etc.

Blend all until smooth.

Per Serving: 175 Calories; 4g Fat; 7g Protein; 32g Carbohydrate; 3g Dietary Fiber.

Granola with fresh fruit

Apple Oat Muffins

Categories   Breads/Cereals

These muffins have a spicy flavor. The apples make them moist, while the oats and raisins provide a nice texture.

Serves   12   Preparation Time 25 min   Total Time 45 min

1 lg	egg, or substitute (see substitution list)
3/4 c	apple juice, or half water and juice
1 c	raisins
1 c	chopped apples
1/2 c	applesauce
1 c	flour
1 c	quick oats
1/3 c	fructose
1 T	baking powder
1 t	salt
2 t	cinnamon

Mix dry and wet ingredients separately. Combine and mix until well moistened. Fill a lightly greased muffin tin to 2/3 full. Bake at 400 for 15-20 minutes. Cool and slice into 12 pieces.

Per Serving:: 133 Calories; 1g Fat; 2g Protein; 32g Carbohydrate; 1g Dietary Fiber.

Banana Bread

Categories   Breads/Cereals

Serve this bread for breakfast or snack time. It's great for parties topped with soy cream cheese.

Serves   12   Yields 1 loaf   Preparation Time 10 minutes
                                    Total Time 1 hour 15 min

1/3 c	fructose
1/2 c	oil
1 T	baking powder
1 t	baking soda
1 1/4 c	whole wheat flour
2 lg	eggs, or substitute (substitution list)
2 med	bananas, mashed
1 T	rice milk, + 1 T vinegar
3/4 t	vanilla
3/4 t	salt

Mix wet ingredients and dry separately. Combine and mix well.
Pour into a loaf pan sprayed with Pam. Bake at 350 for 1 hour.
You may also add walnuts or sunflower seeds.

*Per Serving:: 184 Calories; 10g Fat; 3g Protein;
22g Carbohydrate; 2g Dietary Fiber*

Basic Pancakes

Categories   Breads/Cereals

Use whole grain flour such as Kamut, whole wheat, spelt or replace 1/2 the flour with oats. May also add nuts, seeds, raisin or fruit such as blueberries, rehydrated fruit, or slice bananas and place on to of each pancake before flipping.

Serves 3   Yields 6 pancakes   Preparation Time 20 minutes

3/4 c	soy milk
1 lg	egg, or substitute (see substitution list)
1/4 c	applesauce, or oil
1 c	whole grain flour
2 T	fructose
2 t	baking powder
1/4 t	salt

Mix wet and dry ingredients separately. Add wet ingredients to dry and mix until large lumps disappear. Cook over medium heat until light brown on each side.

Per Serving:: 241 Calories; 3g Fat; 9g Protein; 48g Carbohydrate; 6g Dietary Fiber

Basic Waffles

Categories   Breads/Cereals

Use any whole grain flour. Kamut is especially good and packed with protein. Top with Fresh Fruit Syrup recipe, fresh fruit, apple butter or pure maple syrup.

Serves 4   Yields 8 waffles   Preparation Time 30 minutes

2 c	whole grain flour
1 T	fructose
1 T	baking powder
1 t	salt
1 lg	egg, or substitute (see substitution list)
2 c	soy milk
1/3 c	applesauce, or use oil (higher in fat), or another substitute

Mix wet ingredients in a small bowl. Mix dry ingredients in a large bowl. Add wet ingredients to dry and mix until large lumps disappear. Cook in preheated waffle iron.

Per Serving:: 295 Calories; 5g Fat; 13g Protein; 56g Carbohydrate; 9g Dietary Fiber

Blueberry Oat Muffins

Categories   Breads/Cereals

For a variety, try different berries. These muffins are sweet enough to eat plain. The cinnamon topping is optional.

Serves   12   Preparation Time 15 min   Total Time 45 min

1 1/4 c	oats
1 1/4 c	flour
1/3 c	fructose
1T	baking powder
1/2 t	salt
1 c	rice milk, + 1 T. vinegar
1 lg	egg, or substitute (see substitution list)
1/4 c	oil
3/4 c	blueberries, fresh or frozen

Topping

2 T	fructose
2 t	cinnamon

Lightly spray a muffin pan. In a bowl mix oats, flour, fructose, baking powder, salt, and egg. In another bowl mix rice milk and oil. Add to dry ingredients. Mix until moistened. Fold in blueberries. Fill muffin pan 2/3 full. Mix topping and sprinkle on top. Bake 20 - 25 minutes at 350.

Per Serving: 209 Calories; 6g Fat; 4g Protein; 36g Carbohydrate; 3g Dietary Fiber

Bread Bowls

Categories   Breads/Cereals

When filled with your favorite salad or thick soup, this recipe is a meal in itself. Serve with a light dessert.

Serves 4

Preparation Time - Time to bake the bread depending on whether you use prepared dough or made from scratch.

Make dough for one loaf of whole wheat bread. (see Whole Wheat Bread recipe, or use your favorite recipe or prepared dough.

After making the dough let rise once. Knead and divide into 4 pieces. Roll into 4 circles. Spray the back of 4 oven-safe soup or cereal size bowls with Pam. Place bowls upside down on a cookie sheet. Place circles over the bottom of the bowls. In a pre-heated oven, bake 10 minutes at 375. Remove dough from bowls and turn the dough right side up and set back on cookie sheet. Place back in oven and bake until done (approx. 20 more minutes). Remove from oven and cool for 20 minutes. Place bread bowls in a plastic bag while still warm to keep soft until ready to use.

For the nutritional analysis, see the whole wheat bread recipe.

Burger Buns

Categories   Breads/Cereals

Use these buns for veggie burgers, sloppy Joes, or any sandwiches.

Serves   10   Preparation Time 10 minutes   Total Time 1 hour

1 c + 3 T	warm water
1/3 c	oil
1/8 c	fructose
2 t	yeast
1 lg	egg, or substitute (see substitution list)
3 1/3 c	whole wheat flour
1 t	salt

Combine warm water, oil, fructose, and yeast. Mix and let rest 15 minutes. Add rest and mix well. Roll dough into 1/2 thickness. Cut into round circles about 4 in diameter. A clean, empty can may be used. Place buns on a lightly greased cookie sheet. Lightly brush tops with melted butter or olive oil. Let rise at room temperature for 20 minutes. Bake for 10-20 minutes or until light brown at 400.

Per Serving: 217 Calories; 8g Fat; 6g Protein; 33g Carbohydrate; 5g Dietary Fiber

Granola

Categories   Breads/Cereals

This low-fat version contains no oil. Vary the granola with different dried fruit, nuts, or seeds. Use as a breakfast cereal - hot or cold. Sprinkle over yogurt or frozen Rice/Soy Dream or another dairy free frozen dessert.

Serves 24   Yields 12 cups   Preparation Time 10 minutes
                                 Total Time 45 minutes

8 c	rolled oats
2 c	bran flakes, or other flake cereal
1/2 c	sesame seeds
3/4 c	nuts (walnuts, almonds, pecans, etc.)
3/4 c	sunflower seeds, and/or pumpkin seeds raw, hulled
2 c	raisins, or any dried fruit such as apples, coconut, figs, cranberries, etc.
1 12-oz can	apple juice concentrate
1 c	honey
1 t	vanilla

Heat oven to 300. Lightly spray 3 or 4   9 X 13 pans. In a large bowl combine oats, bran flakes, and sesame seeds. In a medium sauce pan, mix apple juice and honey. Heat until well blended. Pour over oat mixture and mix until well coated. Spread evenly in the 9 X 13 pans. Bake for 30 minutes, stirring every 10 minutes. Cool and stir occasionally breaking up large clumps. Sit out for 3 or 4 days stirring occasionally until dry. Add nuts, dried fruit, etc. Store in gallon jars.

Per Serving: 239 Calories; 7g Fat; 7g Protein; 42g Carbohydrate; 7g Dietary Fiber

Healthy Grain Bread

Categories   Breads/Cereals

This bread recipe can be used in your bread machine or follow the directions for baking it by hand. It is great for breakfast, a snack, or with a meal.

Serves   6   Yields 1 loaf   Preparation Time 20 minutes

1 1/4 c	water, warm
1/4 c	carrots, grated
1/4 c	zucchini, grated
1 T	fructose
2 T	olive oil
2 c	whole wheat flour
1 c	flour
1 1/2 t	salt
1/2 c	bran flakes cereal
1/2 c	raisins
1/3 c	sunflower seeds
2 t	yeast

In a large bowl add warm water and yeast and let sit for a few minutes. Add fructose and bran flakes to soak for a minute. Add the rest of the ingredients and knead for 5 minutes. Let rise until double. Punch down and place in a lightly greased bread pan. Let rise again. Bake at 350 until done - about 35-45 minutes.
*For a bread machine, just add all of the ingredients at once.

Per Serving: 176 Calories; 5g Fat; 5g Protein; 30g Carbohydrate; 4g Dietary Fiber

Heavenly French Toast

Categories   Breads/Cereals

This French toast is light, not greasy, and cholesterol free. You can also add a mashed up banana to the mixture and reduce the tofu.

Serves 4   Preparation Time 30 minutes

1 c	soy milk, or rice milk
3 oz	tofu, lite, silken
2 T	flour
2 T	maple syrup
3/4 t	vanilla
1/2 t	cinnamon
1/4 t	allspice
8 pieces	whole grain bread, sliced

Blend all ingredients, except bread, in a blender until smooth. Quickly dip bread on each side and fry on a dry pan until lightly browned.

Per Serving: 259 Calories; 5g Fat; 12g Protein; 45g Carbohydrate; 7g Dietary Fiber

Herbed Croutons

Categories   Breads/Cereals

Use day-old bread or any type of bread you like. You can blend any of your favorite herbs.

Serves   12   Preparation Time 15 min   Total Time 35 min

4 c	bread cubes
2 T	basil, fresh
1 T	parsley, fresh
1 T	rosemary, fresh
1 t	garlic powder
	or you can use 1 T. dried Italian in place of the 4 seasonings.

Lightly spray a baking sheet. Toss bread with spices. Bake at 350 until light brown and crisp, about 20 minutes.

Per Serving: 43 Calories; 1g Fat; 1g Protein; 8g Carbohydrate; 1g Dietary Fiber

Maple Nut Muffins

Categories   Breads/Cereals

These muffins are a super treat - for breakfast or snack time.

Serves   12   Preparation Time 15 min   Total Time 45 min

1 1/2 c	flour
1 T	baking powder
1/4 t	salt
pinch	allspice
1 lg	egg, or substitute (see substitution list)
1/3 c	rice milk, + 1 T. vinegar
1/2 c	maple syrup
1/2 c	applesauce, or oil
1 c	nuts, chopped (pecans or walnuts)
1 t	vanilla

Mix dry and wet ingredients separately.   Combine with nuts and mix until moistened.   Fill a lightly sprayed muffin tin 2/3 full. Bake 400 for 15-20 minutes.

Per Serving: 183 Calories; 7g Fat; 4g Protein; 27g Carbohydrate; 2g Dietary Fiber

Multi-grain Bread

Categories   Breads/Cereals

This a heavier bread great for sandwiches or toast for breakfast. You can use any kind of multi-grain cereal like 7-grain, 9-grain, etc. Add nuts, seeds, or dried fruit.

Serves   24   Yields 2 loaves   Preparation Time 15 minutes
                                   Total Time 1 hour

1 1/2 c	boiling water
1 c	multi-grain cereal
6 T	oil, or substitute
1/2 c	honey
2 t	salt
1/2 c	warm water
2 t	yeast
1 lg	egg, or substitute (see substitution list)
5 1/2 c	whole wheat flour

Pour boiling water over cereal in a large bowl. Dissolve yeast in warm water. When cereal is luke warm, add yeast and remaining ingredients holding back 3 c flour. Beat 2 minutes. Add in the rest of the flour. Divide dough in half and spread into bottom of loaf pans sprayed with Pam. Let rise until double. Bake at 375 for 50 minutes.

Per Serving: 179 Calories; 5g Fat; 5g Protein; 33g Carbohydrate; 5g Dietary Fiber

Multi-grain muffins

Categories   Breads/Cereals

You can vary these muffins by adding dried fruit, nuts, seeds, carob chips, drained pineapple, mashed bananas, spices, etc.

Serves   24   Preparation Time 15   Total Time 45 minutes

2 c	flour
1 1/2 c	7 or 9-grain cereal
1/3 c	fructose
1/2 t	salt
1 T	baking powder
2 c	rice milk, + 1 T vinegar
1 lg	egg, or substitute (see substitution list)
1/3 c	oil

Mix dry ingredients and wet ingredients separately. Then mix together. Fill a lightly sprayed muffin tin about 2/3 full with batter. Bake about 30 minutes at 375 until lightly brown.

Per Serving: 139 Calories; 4g Fat; 3g Protein; 24g Carbohydrate; 3g Dietary Fiber

Multi-Grain Pancakes/Waffles

Categories   Breads/Cereals

This hearty bread is loaded with protein and fiber. Try different whole grains such as Kamut or spelt. Top with homemade syrup (see Fruit Juice/Jelly recipe), fresh fruit, or preserves.

Serves 4   Yields 8   Preparation Time 10 min
                                Total Time 30 minutes

3/4 c	whole wheat flour
1/2 c	flour, (or other whole grain flour)
1/8 c	flax seed, ground
1/8 c	corn meal
1/8 c	fructose, (or honey, maple syrup, etc)
2 t	baking powder
1 t	salt
1 lg	egg, or substitute (see substitution list)
1 1/4 c	soy milk
1/4 c	applesauce, or oil (waffles may need a little more oil to prevent sticking)

In a large bowl, mix dry ingredients. In a small bowl mix wet ingredients. Add to dry ingredients and mix until large lumps are gone. Cook over medium heat on a non-stick pan.

Per Serving: 246 Calories; 5g Fat; 9g Protein; 44g Carbohydrate; 6g Dietary Fiber

Naturally Leavened Pancakes

Categories   Breads/Cereals

You do not need any yeast, baking powder, or soda for these pancakes. They are great on a camping trip!

Serves 8   Yields 12   Preparation Time 5 minutes

2 c	whole grain flour
2 c	water
1/2 t	salt
1/2 T	oil

Mix in a large bowl. Whip batter. Let stand at least 1 hour or over night.

Per Serving: 146 Calories; 2g Fat; 5g Protein;
29g Carbohydrate; 5g Dietary Fiber

Oatmeal Wheat Bread

Categories   Breads/Cereals

Although this is a heavier bread, it is low in fat. It is great for breakfast or as a snack. Top with nut butter or preserves.

Serves   24   Yields 2 loaves   Preparation Time 20 minutes
                                  Total 1 hour 30 minutes

1 c	oats
2 c	boiling water
2 T	oil, or substitute
1 c	warm water
2 t	yeast
1/2 c	honey, or molasses
2 t	salt
5 c	whole wheat flour

To the boiling water add the oats and oil. Let soak and cool. To the warm water add the yeast and let set 5 minutes. In a large bowl, add all ingredients. Mix well. Dough will be sticky. Add more flour if necessary. Let rise. Punch down and put into 2 lightly sprayed loaf pans. Let rise again. Bake at 350 for 45 minutes.

Per Serving: 153 Calories; 2g Fat; 4g Protein; 30g Carbohydrate; 2g Dietary Fiber

Old Fashioned Cornbread

Categories   Breads/Cereals

This basic cornbread recipe can be used in a muffin pan, 8 X 8 baking pan, or topping for Tamale Pie type recipes.

Serves   9 -12   Preparation Time 10 minutes
                         Total Time 30 minutes

3/4 c	corn meal
1 1/4 c	whole wheat flour, or white flour
2 T	fructose, or honey
1 1/2 T	baking powder
1 t	salt
1/4 c	oil, or applesauce, or substitute
1 lg	egg, or substitute (see substitution list
1 c	rice milk, + 1 T. vinegar

Mix dry and wet ingredients separately. Add wet ingredients to dry and blend until large lumps disappear. Lightly spray an 8 pan or 12 -muffin pan. Bake at 400 for 20-25 minutes. Cool and cut into 9 pieces.

Per Serving: 176 Calories; 7g Fat; 3g Protein;
27g Carbohydrate; 3g Dietary Fiber

Pizza Dough – Whole wheat

Categories   Breads/Cereals

Top with any pesto sauce or your favorite tomato or pizza sauce.
Layer any vegetables you wish. You can also fold it in half and
stuff it for a calzone. To save time, use a bread machine and set
on the dough setting.

Serves 4   Total Time 1 hour 45 minutes.

3/4 c	warm water
1 pkg	dry yeast, (or use the sour dough starter)
1 T	olive oil
1/2 t	salt
1 1/2 c	whole wheat flour

Mix water and yeast until dissolved. Mix in oil and salt. Add
flour - you may need to add up to 1/2 c more flour if dough is too
sticky. Knead for 5 minutes. Put in greased bowl and let rise 1
hour or until doubled. Roll out to a 12" circle. Bake on a baking
stone or a lightly sprayed pizza pan. Bake at 425 for 10 minutes.
Add sauce and toppings and bake another 10 minutes. Add
grated soy cheese and bake another 10 minutes (opt). Cut into 8
slices.

Per Serving: 274 Calories; 5g Fat; 7g Protein;
49g Carbohydrate; 2g Dietary Fiber

Poppy Seed Muffins

Categories   Breads/Cereals

The poppy seeds and almonds give these muffins a nice crunch.

Serves 12   Yields 12   Preparation Time 20 minutes
                              Total Time 40 minutes

2 c	whole wheat flour (or a mix of flours)
1/2 c	fructose
1/4 c	applesauce or oil
1/2 t	orange peel, grated
1 lg	egg or substitute
1 T	baking powder
1/2 t	salt
1/4 t	almond extract
1 c	rice milk + 1T. vinegar
1/2 c	almonds, chopped
3 T	poppy seeds

Mix dry and wet ingredients separately. Then combine and mix
until well moistened. Fill a lightly sprayed muffin tin about 3/4
full. Bake at 400 for 20 minutes.

*Per Serving: 180 Calories; 5g Fat; 5g Protein;
32g Carbohydrate; 3g Dietary Fiber*

Soft Whole Wheat Flour Tortillas

Categories   Breads/Cereals

*Once you eat homemade tortillas, store bought will never do.
Use with any sandwich fillings, burrito mix or as a compliment
to any dish.*

Serves   18   Yields 18   Preparation Time 10 minutes
                                  Total Time 1 hour

6 c	flour, (whole wheat, white, spelt, or a combination, etc)
2 t	salt
2 t	baking powder
1/2 c	oil, or softened Spectrum shortening
2 c	warm water

Mix dry ingredients. Pour in oil and mix well, or cut in softened
shortening until crumbly. Pour in warm water and mix dough
into a ball and knead for 1 minute. Let dough rest 10 minutes.
Divide into 18 balls and roll out thin. Cook on dry, non-stick pan
over medium heat until they start to brown. Flip and cook the
other side. Approximately 30 seconds to 1 minute per side.

*Per Serving: 142 Calories; 5g Fat; 4g Protein;
22g Carbohydrate; 4g Dietary Fiber*

Tropical Cornbread

Categories   Breads/Cereals

Serve with soups, stews, casseroles, or salads. It will compliment most dishes. For an after dinner treat, top with honey or preserves.

Serves   16   Preparation Time 10 min Total Time 35 minutes

1 c	cornmeal
1 c	flour
1 1/2 T	baking powder
1 lg	egg, or substitute (see substitution list)
1/2 c	rice milk, + 1 T. vinegar
1/2 c	pineapple, pureed
1/2 c	honey, (or 1/3 cup fructose)
1/2 c	dried coconut
1/4 c	oil, or substitute (see substitution list)
1/2 t	salt

Heat oven to 375. Lightly spray an 8 X 8 square pan with vegetable spray. In a large bowl mix dry ingredients and coconut. In a smaller bowl mix egg, milk, honey, pineapple, and oil. Add to the dry ingredients. Pour into the pan and sprinkle with a little coconut if desired. Bake for 20 – 25 minutes.

Per Serving: 145 Calories; 5g Fat; 2g Protein; 24g Carbohydrate; 1g Dietary Fiber

Whole Grain Country Biscuits

Categories   Breads/Cereals

Refrigerator store bought biscuits jus can't compete with these warm "home-style" biscuits. They are wonderful for every occasion. They are fast and easy to make.

Serves   20   Yields 20   Preparation Time 10 minutes
                                  Total Time 30 minutes

3 c	whole grain flour
4 1/2 t	baking powder
2 T	fructose, or honey
1/2 t	salt
3/4 t	cream of tartar
1/3 c	oil, or substitute (see substitution list), softened Spectrum shortening (see pantry list)
1 lg	egg, or substitute (see substitution list)
1 c	rice milk, or soy milk, + 1 T. vinegar

In large bowl, mix flour, powder, fructose, salt, tarter. Pour in oil and mix well. Add egg and milk. Knead for 2-3 minutes. Roll to 1" thick and cut to 2" circles. Using an ungreased pan, place biscuits 1" apart. Bake at 375 for 20-25 minutes or until lightly browned.

Per Serving: 110 Calories; 4g Fat; 3g Protein; 16g Carbohydrate; 2g Dietary Fiber

Whole Grain Muffins

Categories   Breads/Cereals

This is a basic muffin recipe. Add any nuts, seeds, or fruit you wish to vary the flavor and texture.

Serves   12   Yields 12   Preparation Time 10 minutes
                                            Total Time 45 minutes

2 c	wheat flour, or whole grain flour
1 T	baking powder
1 t	baking soda
1/2 t	salt
1/4 c	fructose
1 1/2 c	rice milk, + 1 T. vinegar
2 T	applesauce
1 lg	egg, or substitute (see substitution list)
3 T	water

Mix dry and wet ingredients separately. Then mix together and add any nuts, seeds or fruit, and stir until blended. Lightly spray a 12 muffin pan. Fill 2/3 full. Bake at 400 for 30 minutes.

Per Serving: 113 Calories; 1g Fat; 3g Protein;
25g Carbohydrate; 2g Dietary Fiber

Whole Wheat Bread

Categories   Breads/Cereals

This recipe works wonderfully in a bread machine. You can double the recipe to make two loaves if making by hand.

Serves   12   Yields 1 loaf   Preparation Time 30 minutes

1 1/4 c	water, warm
1/8 c	oil
2 T	fructose
1 T	molasses (optional)
3 1/2 c	whole wheat flour
1 1/2 t	salt
1 1/2 T	gluten, wheat
2 t	yeast

Pour warm water in large bowl. Sprinkle with yeast. Let set until yeast is bubbly. Add the rest of the ingredients and knead 5 minutes. Cover and let rise until double. Punch down and knead 5 minutes. Shape into a loaf and place in lightly sprayed bread pan. Cover and let rise again until doubled. Bake at 350 until golden brown and done, approximately 30-45 minutes.

Per Serving: 164 Calories; 3g Fat; 7g Protein;
30g Carbohydrate; 4g Dietary Fiber

Whole Wheat French Bread

Categories   Breads/Cereals

This bread is unbelievably easy, especially if using a bread machine on the dough cycle. You can double the recipe if you are mixing the dough by hand. It is low in fat, as it contains no oil.

Serves   12   Yield 1 loaf   Total 2 hours

3 c	whole wheat flour, or use a mixture of white or other whole grain flours
2 T	fructose
2 t	yeast
1 t	salt
1 1/4 c	warm water

If using a bread machine, place in all ingredients and set the dough cycle. When complete, roll into a long loaf.

If mixing by hand, pour the warm water into a large mixing bowl. Sprinkle yeast on top, and let sit 5 minutes. Add the rest of the ingredients and knead for 5 minutes. Cover and let rise in a warm place until doubled in size. Punch down and knead again for 5 minutes. Roll into a long loaf.

Once you have a long loaf, sprinkle 1/4 cup corn meal on a 9 x 13 sheet pan. Place the loaf on the sheet. Make 3 slices with a sharp knife diagonally across the top. Cover and let rise until doubled. Place in preheated oven at 350 and bake for 25-30 minutes or until done. Cool and place in a plastic bag to keep soft or leave out to harden for a crunchy loaf.

Per Serving: 115 Calories; 1g Fat; 4g Protein;
25g Carbohydrate; 4g Dietary Fiber

Main Dishes

BBQ Tofu with Vegetables and Island Salsa

Acorn Squash with Rice Stuffing

Categories   Main Dishes

*You can use small pumpkins, or other winter squash. Serve with
steamed vegetables.*

Serves   6 (Halves)   Preparation Time 30 minutes
                         Total Time 1 hour

3 sm	winter squash, halved and seeded
2/3 c	vegetable stock
3 lg	mushroom, chopped
1 sm	onion, chopped
2 T	vegetable oil
1 1/2 c	stuffing cubes
1/2 c	corn
1 c	brown and wild rice, cooked
1 t	thyme or sage
	salt and pepper to taste

Heat oven to 350. Place squash face down on a cookie sheet and
bake until almost soft about 30 minutes. Meanwhile, in a skillet,
sauté onion in oil until lightly browned. Transfer to a bowl and
add mushrooms, stuffing, corn, rice, and thyme or sage. Toss.
Pour and mix in vegetable stock (add a little water if necessary to
make a moist stuffing). Add salt and pepper. Spoon into squash.
Cover and bake for about 20 minutes.

*Per Serving:: 330 Calories; 7g Fat; 9g Protein;
58g Carbohydrate; 5g Dietary Fiber*

Autumn Casserole

Categories   Main Dishes

Experiment with other fresh vegetables and herbs. If you are short on time, cut the vegetables the night before, and put all ingredients in a crockpot in the morning. Serve with fresh bread and crisp green salad.

Serves   6   Preparation Time 15 minutes
                           Total Time 1 hour 15 minutes

1 T	olive oil
1 lg	onion, chopped
1 lg	bell pepper, chopped
2 c	eggplant, cubed
3 med	cloves garlic, minced
1 14 oz. can	tomatoes, diced
2 lg	potatoes, cubed
1 t	thyme
1 t	oregano, dried
1 t	salt
1/2 t	pepper

Sauté in the olive oil for 3 minutes onion, bell pepper. Combine all ingredients and put into casserole dish or crock pot. Bake at 350 for 1 hr. (if using a crock pot, cook on low for 8-10 hours or on high for 4-6 hours)

Per Serving: 88 Calories; 3g Fat; 2g Protein; 16g Carbohydrate; 3g Dietary Fiber

Baked Potato Vegetable Parmesan

Categories   Main Dishes

Use your favorite marinara or spaghetti sauce and your favorite mix of steamed veggies to make this a complete meal. To save time, bake potatoes ahead of time.

Serves   1   Preparation Time 10 minutes

1 lg	potato, baked
1/2 c	marinara sauce
1/2 c	mixed vegetables, steamed
1 t	soy parmesan cheese, grated

Potatoes, Marinara sauce and vegetables should be hot. Cut open baked potato and pour Marinara sauce over the top. Top with vegetables and Parmesan cheese. Serve while hot.

Per Serving:: 218 Calories; 4g Fat; 6g Protein; 41g Carbohydrate; 9g Dietary Fiber

Balsamic Vinaigrette Pasta

Categories   Main Dishes

My sister, Lari, originated this recipe because of her love for pasta dishes, and little time to prepare them. For a variation, try different cheeses, nuts, or vegetables (mushrooms, green onions, olives, steamed mixed vegetables). Try other favorite vinegar and oil type salad dressings. Serve as a main dish or as a pasta salad.

Serves   6   Preparation time 30 minutes

8 oz	cooked whole grain pasta, spaghetti, linguini,etc.
1/2 c	chopped tomatoes
1/2 c	artichoke hearts, drained
1/3 c	nuts walnut, pine nuts, peanuts, etc
1/2 c	grated soy cheese, parmesan, or fetta cheese
1/2 c	balsamic vinaigrette dressing (see recipe, or use prepared)

Cook pasta according to directions. Rinse and drain. Add vegetables and mix. Pour over dressing. Heat and serve.

Per Serving: 163 Calories; 15g Fat; 2g Protein; 7g Carbohydrate; 2g Dietary Fiber

BBQ Tofu with Vegetables and Island Salsa

Categories   Main Dishes

This light taste of BBQ gives this dish a gourmet look and great flavor. Top with Island Salsa (see recipe) and garnish with micro greens. You can use any vegetable or a combination. If you don't have a grill lightly fry the tofu and steam the vegetables.

Serves 8 Preparation Time 20 minutes   Total Time 45 min

1 lb	tofu, firm, drained
1/2 c	barbecue sauce
1 bunch	asparagus

Drain tofu and cut into 8 slices. Grill or fry tofu until lightly browned. Grill or steam asparagus until crisp tender. On eight plates place one grilled tofu slice. Top with Island Salsa and micro greens. Drizzle BBQ sauce over all over tofu and around plate.

Per Serving:: 183 Calories; 6g Fat; 12g Protein; 23g Carbohydrate; 4g Dietary Fiber

Eggplant and Zucchini Skillet

Categories   Main Dishes

Serve this hearty casserole with a fresh green salad and fresh bread or with a cooked grain.

Serves 6   Preparation Time 30 minutes

3 c	eggplant, chopped 3/4
1 T	olive oil
3/4 c	onion, chopped
1/2 c	bell pepper, chopped
2 c	zucchini, chopped
1 14-oz can	tomatoes, crushed
1/4 c	basil, fresh
1 t	salt
1/2 t	pepper
2 med	garlic clove, minced

In a medium frying pan, heat oil and add eggplant. Cook until lightly brown. Add onions, bell pepper, cook 5 minutes. Add zucchini and cook 5 minutes. Add tomatoes and 1/2 c water. Simmer until vegetables are just tender. Stir in garlic and basil. Serve hot.

Per Serving: 62 Calories; 3g Fat; 2g Protein; 10g Carbohydrate; 3g Dietary Fiber

Eggplant Parmesan

Categories   Main Dishes

Make your own marinara sauce (see Zesty Marinara Sauce recipe) or use a ready-made one. Serve with whole grain noodles on the side topped with extra marinara sauce and steamed vegetables.

Serves 6   Preparation Time 45 minutes

2 T	soy parmesan cheese, grated
1 med	eggplant, sliced into 12- ½" slices
1 t	paprika
1 c	soy yogurt, add small amount of water to make smooth
1 c	breadcrumbs
1 c	flour
1 t	salt
1 t	black pepper
1 pint	marinara sauce

Using three different bowls, in the first bowl mix flour, salt, pepper, and paprika. In the second bowl mix the soy yogurt and water. In the third bowl the breadcrumbs. For breading the eggplant, first dip into the flour, then the soy yogurt, then the breadcrumbs. After they are coated, bake at 375 until medium brown. Ladle the marinara over eggplant and sprinkle with the parmesan cheese and bake in the oven for 10 minutes or until the cheese is melted and sauce is hot at 350.

If you want crispier eggplant you can fry them in a small amount of olive oil instead of baking them. It will raise the fat content.

Per Serving: 222 Calories; 4g Fat; 7g Protein; 38g Carbohydrate; 3g Dietary Fiber

Garden Burrito

Categories   Main Dishes

Serve these burritos for breakfast, lunch, or dinner.   We love these as Breakfast Burritos along with soy sausage or fresh fruit.

Serves 6   Preparation Time 30 minutes

6 med	tortillas, whole wheat
2 c	hash browns, frozen
1/2 c	bell pepper, chopped
1/2 c	onion, chopped
1 10 oz pkg	mixed vegetables, frozen, broccoli mix or your favorite
1/2 c	tomatoes, chopped
1/2 c	soy cheese, shredded
	salt and pepper to taste

Sauté onion and bell pepper in a small amount of water for 3 minutes. Add the hash browns and mixed vegetables and cook according to hash brown directions. Wrap tortillas in foil and heat in oven. On each tortilla divide equally, potatoes, vegetables, soy cheese, and tomatoes. Wrap up burrito.

Garnish with salsa, soy sour cream, or Bragg's Amino Liquid.

Per Serving: 306 Calories; 6g Fat; 8g Protein; 56g Carbohydrate; 4g Dietary Fiber

Garden Pizza

Categories   Main Dishes

You can make this pizza in the time it takes to buy or bake a prepared one. Serve with a fresh green salad and your favorite dressing.

Serves 4   Preparation Time 15 minutes
                 Total Time 30 min

1 med	pizza crust, prepared or whole wheat flatbread
1 c	pizza sauce, or pesto sauce (see recipes)
1 c	artichoke hearts, canned, drained
1 c	spinach, fresh, chopped
1/4 c	green onions, chopped
1/2 c	zucchini, sliced thin
1/4 c	black olives, chopped
1 c	soy cheese, mozzarella (opt)

Spread sauce over prepared crust. Layer the vegetables. Sprinkle the cheese on top. Bake at 375 for 10-15 minutes until vegetables are soft and cheese is melted.

Depending on the amount of time you have, you can use pre-cooked or prepared pizza crust, pitas, English muffins, or make your own homemade pizza crust (see Pizza Dough recipe). For a variety, try different vegetables.

Per Serving: 406 Calories; 8g Fat; 13g Protein; 72g Carbohydrate; 3g Dietary Fiber

Green Chile Chimi

Categories   Main Dishes

These spicy burritos will be a hit. Serve with a fresh green salad.

Serves 8   Preparation Time 15 min
                             Total Time 30 min

8 med	whole wheat flour tortillas
8 whole	green chilies, opened flat
2 1/2 c	seasoned chili beans, cooked and heated
2 1/2 c	brown rice, cooked, or other whole grain (barley, millet, quinoa)
1/2 c	soy cheese, grated

On each tortilla place the rice, beans, cheese, and one opened green chili. Fold tortilla and tuck in ends. Place on a cookie sheet and bake on 350 until tortilla is crisp and lightly browned, about 10 minutes.

May garnish with soy sour cream, salsa or guacamole.

Per Serving: 551 Calories; 13g Fat; 14g Protein; 96g Carbohydrate; 6g Dietary Fiber

Indonesian Rice and Vegetables with Peanut Gravy

Categories   Main Dishes

This Indonesian recipe is modified to fit a low fat, vegetarian diet. You can use regular coconut milk, low-fat coconut milk or equal amount of rice milk and 1/4 t. coconut extract to reduce the fat content even more.

Serves   12   Preparation Time 45 minutes

2 c ea	carrots, cauliflower, broccoli (leaving stems)
1/2 c	peanuts
6 c	brown rice, cooked and hot

In a large skillet simmer vegetables in the coconut milk (reserving 1/2 cup liquid) until tender. Meanwhile make gravy. Serve the vegetables over the rice and pour the gravy over all.

Gravy

1/2 c	onion, diced
1 T	olive oil
3 med	garlic clove, minced
4 T	peanut butter
4 T	hot water
1 1/2 c	coconut milk - lite
2 T	lemon juice
	dash cayenne pepper or to taste

Sauté onion and garlic in oil until soft. Add in peanut butter and hot water and stir until smooth. Simmer 5 minutes. Add cayenne, lemon juice, coconut milk to make the desired consistency:

Per Serving: 458 Calories; 11g Fat; 11g Protein; 80g Carbohydrate; 4g Dietary Fiber

Jambalaya

Categories   Main Dishes

This is a spicy, vegetarian version of a southern tradition. This thick stew can be served with baked yams or sweet potatoes and fresh bread.

Serves 4   Preparation Time 15 min
                             Total Time 1 hr. 15 min

3 T	water
1/2 c	onion, chopped
1/2 c	mushrooms, chopped
2 lg	garlic clove, minced
1/2 c	bell pepper, chopped
1/2 c	celery, chopped
2 T	Bragg's amino liquids
1 14-oz can	tomatoes, chopped
1 c	brown rice, raw
2 c	water
1/2 t	thyme
1/2 t	paprika
2 T	parsley, fresh
1/4 t	red chili powder
1/4 t	pepper
1/2 t	salt

Sauté onions, bell pepper, celery in water until soft. Add garlic and mushrooms and cook 5 minutes. Add rest of the ingredients and mix well. Pour into a lightly sprayed casserole dish. Bake at 350 for 1 hour or until rice is tender, and water is absorbed.

Per Serving: 219 Calories; 2g Fat; 6g Protein; 37g Carbohydrate; 3g Dietary Fiber

Pasta with Broccoli Pesto

Categories   Main Dishes

Use any shape pasta. Rainbow, fettuccini, or bow ties work great. Serve with whole wheat French bread and a fresh green salad.

Serves 6   Yields 8 cups   Preparation Time 30 minutes

1 lb	broccoli florets, (about 4 c)
3 med	garlic clove, minced
1/3 c	soy parmesan cheese, grated
3T	olive oil
1/2 t	salt
12 oz	pasta, whole grain
1c	tomato, chopped
1/2 c	liquid from broccoli

Cover and cook broccoli in 1 cup water until tender, drain reserving liquid. In a blender, combine broccoli, parmesan cheese, olive oil, salt, and 1/4 c. reserved liquid. Blend until smooth. Add more liquid if needed to make desired consistency. Add garlic and pulse until mixed (2-3 seconds). Cook and drain pasta. Add pesto and mix gently. Garnish with tomatoes.

Per Serving: 288 Calories; 8g Fat; 11g Protein; 49g Carbohydrate; 7g Dietary Fiber

Rice and Eggplant Stuffed Peppers

Categories   Main Dishes

A hearty main dish loaded with flavor and texture.   You can replace the rice with any whole cooked grains or a combination.

Serves 4   Preparation Time 30 minutes
                 Total Time 1 hr 15 min

4 med	bell pepper
1 T	olive oil
1/2 c	onion, chopped
1 lg	garlic clove, minced
1 sm	eggplant, cut 1/2 thick
1/2 c	breadcrumbs
1/2 c	brown rice, cooked
1/4 c	soy parmesan cheese, grated
1/3 c	parsley, fresh
1/4 c	basil, fresh
4 T	catsup

Sauté onion in oil until soft. Add eggplant, cover and cook 8 minutes. Add garlic and cook 1 minute. Stir in bread crumbs, rice, cheese, herbs and mix well. Cut off tops of peppers and remove seeds. Stuff each pepper with rice filling. Place peppers in a small baking dish filled with 1/2 inch of water. Top each with 1 T. catsup. Cover and bake at 350 for 45 minutes.

Per Serving: 288 Calories; 7g Fat; 8g Protein; 53g Carbohydrate; 8g Dietary Fiber

Savory Lentil Loaf

Categories   Main Dishes

We love this lentil loaf recipe. You can make it using your own seasonings that you use for meat loaf only replace the meat with cooked lentils. Serve with a fresh garden salad or coleslaw and Roasted Potatoes.

Serves   12   Preparation Time 15 min
                            Total Time 1 hr 15 min

2 c	lentils, cooked
1 c	brown rice, cooked
1 c	oats
1/2 c ea.	onion, celery, carrots, chopped or grated
1	egg, beaten
1/2 c	spaghetti sauce (or tomato, catsup, BBQ sauce
1 t	garlic powder or fresh chopped garlic
1/2 t ea.	sage, marjoram, salt
1/4 t	pepper

Coarsely mash lentils and rice. Add the rest and mix well and form into a loaf. Spray a loaf pan with vegetable spray and place mixture in pan. Smooth out top. May spoon extra sauce on the top. Bake uncovered at 350 for 45 minutes to 1 hour. Cool 5 minutes. Turn out on platter.

Per Serving: 107 Calories; 2g Fat; 6g Protein; 15g Carbohydrate;4 g Dietary Fiber

Stuffed Manicotti with Marinara

Categories   Main Dishes

You can stuff manicotti or the large shell pasta. Serve with fresh mixed greens with raspberry vinaigrette.

Serves 6   Preparation Time 20 minutes   Total Time 1 hr

1 10-oz pkg	spinach, thawed and drained
1 1/2 c	tofu lite, firm, mashed
1 med	onion, chopped
2 lg	garlic clove, minced
1 med	zucchini, grated
1 16-oz pkg	manicotti, whole grain
2 c	marinara sauce, prepared, or see recipe
1 c	soy cheese, mozzarella style

Sauté onion. And zucchini in 3 T. water until soft. Add garlic and sauté 1 minute. Add spinach and tofu. Mix and stuff pasta. Place in a casserole dish. Pour Marinara sauce over the top of the pasta. Cover and bake for 30 - 45 minutes at 350. Sprinkle the soy mozzarella cheese over the top the last 10 minutes.

Per Serving: 351 Calories; 3g Fat; 13g Protein; 68g Carbohydrate; 5g Dietary Fiber

Stuffing and Vegetable Casserole

Categories   Main Dishes

This casserole is a great main dish for a vegetarian Thanksgiving or anytime of the year.

Serves   12   Preparation Time 15 minutes   Total Time 1 hr.

1 10-oz pkg	stuffing cubes, herbed seasoned
1/4 c	soy margarine, or butter - melted
2 T	"chickenles"s broth powder + 3/4 cup water, or
use	prepared (see Pantry list)
2 14-oz cans	cream of mushroom soup, or cream of "chidkenless" soup mix and water, or other prepared cream soup
1 12-oz pkg	mixed vegetables, frozen, or green beans or broccoli
1 c	soy cheese, grated (optional)

In a bowl, mix water and broth powder. Add stuffing and melted soy margarine. Mix until moist. Spread into a lightly sprayed 9 X 13 pan. In a bowl mix soup, and vegetables. Spread over stuffing. Cover and bake 45 minutes at 350. Sprinkle with cheese and bake until cheese is melted.

Per Serving: 211 Calories; 8g Fat; 8g Protein; 29g Carbohydrate; 3g Dietary Fiber

Sweet and Sour Tempeh Kabobs

Categories   Main Dishes

Kabobs are colorful and fun to it. Serve with fresh asparagus for a complete meal.

Serves 6   Preparation Time 40 minutes   Total time 1 hour

1 med	onion, cut in large chunks
1 c	cherry tomatoes, whole
1 c	mushrooms, whole
4 med	carrots, sliced 1/2 thick
2 med	bell peppers, cut in chunks
1 sm	zucchini, sliced 1/2-inch thick
1 sm	summer squash, sliced 1/2 thick
1 14-oz can	pineapple chunks in juice, reserve juice (if
1 8-oz pkg	tempeh, pre-cooked
1 c	sweet and sour sauce, see recipe or use prepared
4 c	brown rice, cooked or other cooked whole grain

12 wooden skewers soaked in water at least 20 minutes

Steam vegetables until crisp tender. Cool enough to handle.
Meanwhile, cut tempeh into 1/2 to 1 inch cubes. Sauté tempeh in
1 T. peanut oil until light brown. Alternate vegetables with
pineapple and tempeh and place on wet skewers. Lay on a
baking sheet and baste with some of the sweet and sour sauce.
Use a BBQ grill or place in 425 oven and grill or broil for 10
minutes on each side.

To serve, place 1 c. cooked rice on a plate. Lay 2-3 kabobs on
the rice. Ladle sauce over kabobs and rice. Serve hot.

*Per Serving: 337 Calories; 4g Fat; 13g Protein;
66g Carbohydrate; 7g Dietary Fiber*

Sweet and Sour Tofu Stir-fry

Categories   Main Dishes

You can pour this stir-fry over any cooked whole grains or over cooked noodles sautéed one minute in olive oil and garlic.

Serves 8   Preparation Time 30 minutes

1 12-oz pkg	tofu, firm, Chinese style
2 lg	garlic cloves, minced
2 t	ginger root, grated
3 T	sesame oil
1 lg	onion, cut in chunks
3 med	carrots, sliced thin
2 lg	celery stalk, sliced thin
1 c	pineapple chunks in juice, reserve juice
2 c	brown rice, cooked

In a large wok or skillet, stir-fry tofu and ginger in oil until tofu is lightly browned. Remove from wok and drain on paper towel. To wok, add garlic, onion, carrots, celery, and stir-fry 5 minutes (add a little water to prevent sticking if necessary). Add pineapple and cabbage and stir-fry until cabbage is wilted. Return tofu to wok and heat through.

Sauce

Use the **Sweet and Sour Sauce** recipe or used prepared.   Pour over vegetables and cook until sauce thickens (approx. 2 min.). Serve over hot, cooked rice

Per Serving: 206 Calories; 8g Fat; 15g Protein; 32g Carbohydrate; 2g Dietary Fiber

Teriyaki Tofu Pasta

Categories   Main Dishes

Teriyaki is a traditional Japanese flavor. For a more Chinese flavor use soy sauce or Bragg's Amino Liquid. Serve with a green salad and whole wheat French bread

Serves 4   Yields 3 cups   Preparation Time 30 minutes

1 8-oz pkg	pasta, whole grain (spaghetti, linguini, fettuccini, etc.)
1 c	tofu block, Chinese style, julienned
3 lg	green onion, sliced
2 med	celery stalks, julienned
1 c	spinach, chopped (or chard, etc.)
1 T	peanut oil
4 T	teriyaki sauce
1/2 t	red pepper flakes
3 lg	garlic cloves, minced

Cook pasta according to directions. Sauté celery and onions in olive oil until soft (about 5 minutes). Add tofu and sauté until lightly browned. Add spinach and sauté 3 more minutes. Add garlic and sauté for 1 minute. Add cooked pasta, teriyaki sauce, and pepper flakes. Toss and serve.

Per Serving: 292 Calories; 7g Fat; 14g Protein; 49g Carbohydrate; 6g

Three Sisters Stew

Categories   Main Dishes

Native Americans referred to these 3 vegetables (beans, corn and squash) as the 3 Sisters as they were the main staples. This hearty vegetable stew is great for cooler weather. Serve with cornbread or tortillas and a fresh green salad.

Serves 8   Preparation Time 15 minutes   Total Time 45 min

2 T	olive oil
1 c	onion, chopped
2 lg	garlic cloves, minced
1 14-oz can	tomatoes, diced
1/2 c	water
2 c	beans, cooked (pintos, black, or kidney)
1 T	basil, fresh
1 t	oregano
1/2 c	bell pepper, chopped
2 c	winter squash, peeled and chopped
3/4 c	corn
	salt and pepper to taste

Sauté onion and bell pepper in oil for 3 minutes. Add tomatoes and cook 3 minutes. Add beans, water, basil, oregano, garlic, and salt and pepper. Simmer 20 minutes. Add squash and corn and simmer 10 minutes.

Per Serving: 249 Calories; 4g Fat; 13g Protein; 42g Carbohydrate; 15g Dietary Fiber

Vegetarian Lo Mien

Categories   Main Dishes

Serve with steamed rice or the Fried Rice recipe. Save time by using a large bag of frozen vegetables (Oriental style). Cook 5 minutes with very little water.

Serves 4   Preparation Time 20 minutes   Total Time 40 min

2 T	olive oil
2 lg	garlic cloves, minced
1 t	ginger root, grated
2 c	cabbage, chopped
1/2 c	green onion, sliced into long slivers
2 c	zucchini, julienned, or other vegetables
1 c	snow pea pods, fresh, sliced
2 c	broccoli, chopped, or asparagus
4 c	noodles, whole grain, cooked and drained
1 c	water
2 T	cornstarch, or arrowroot powder
1/2 c	teriyaki sauce (or use soy sauce, or Bragg's Amino Liquids for less sweet flavor)

In1T. olive oil, sauté broccoli, onion, garlic, and ginger until broccoli is bright green. Add zucchini, snow peas, and cabbage. Sauté about 5 more minutes. Mix teriyaki sauce with 1 c water and cornstarch. Pour over vegetables, simmer until crisp tender and sauce thickens.

Meanwhile, sauté garlic one minute in the other 1 T. olive oil. Add cooked noodles and stir to coat and heat. Divide noodles on 4 plates. Spoon vegetables over top. Serve at once.

Per Serving: 292 Calories; 9g Fat; 11g Protein;
45g Carbohydrate; 5g Dietary Fiber

Egg Rolls with Plum Salsa

Autumn Stuffed Pumpkin

Categories   Side Dishes / Vegetables

A fun and attractive side dish and/or centerpiece while fresh pumpkins are available. For individual side dishes, use 6-8 small pumpkins.

Serves 8-10 - if one med. Pumpkin   Preparation Time 30 min
                                        Total Time 1 hour 15 min

1 med	pumpkin
4 c	apples, sliced
2 c	raisins
2 T	butter, softened or use olive oil
1 t	cinnamon
1/4 t	cloves
4 T	brown sugar (or 4 T. fructose + 1 T maple syrup)

Cut top off pumpkin and save. Scoop out seeds. Spread the inside of the pumpkin with the butter (or coat with olive oil) and sprinkle with salt. Mix the rest of the ingredients together and spoon into pumpkin. Put lid on pumpkin. Place in pan containing 1-2 water. Bake at 375 for 1 hour or until Pumpkin is soft. Scoop out pumpkin as you serve up.

*Per Serving:: 151 Calories; 3g Fat; 1g Protein;
34g Carbohydrate; 3g Dietary Fiber*

Baked Beans

Categories   Side Dishes / Vegetables

These beans have a spicy yet sweet taste. If you have the time, start with dried beans and simmer until almost soft, then follow the directions. This way you can make a large pot and freeze some for later.

Serves   8   Preparation Time 10 minutes   Total Time 1 hour

4 c	canned, unseasoned beans (adzuki, lima, navy, kidney, etc.), rinsed and drained
1/2 c	water
1/2 c	onion, chopped
1 T	molasses
1 t	dry mustard
1/2 t	salt

Pour into a large baking dish or crock pot. Add the rest of the ingredients and cover and bake about 45 minutes. Add extra water if needed during baking.

Per Serving:: 186 Calories; 1g Fat; 12g Protein; 34g Carbohydrate; 13g Dietary Fiber;

Breaded Vegetables

Categories   Side Dishes / Vegetables

Use a variety of your favorite vegetables such as summer squash, onions, or eggplant. Top with marinara sauce, salad dressing, or vegetable dip.

Serves 4   Preparation Time 20 minutes

2 c	vegetables, assorted, fresh and sliced 1/2 thick
1 c	flour
1 c	seasoned breadcrumbs
1/3 c	sesame seeds
1 t	chili powder
1 c	soy yogurt, thinned with water

Put flour in a small bowl, the thinned yogurt in another bowl and the bread crumbs in another bowl. Dip each vegetable slice in flour, then yogurt, then bread crumbs. Fry in a small amount of olive or peanut oil.

For a lower fat version skip the yogurt and flour. Lay vegetables on baking sheet, brush one side with olive oil. Using the bread crumb mixture, sprinkle a thin coat of crumbs on each vegetable. Bake for 10 minutes on 425.   Turn and brush with olive oil and sprinkle more crumb mixture and bake for 10 more minutes.

Per Serving: 295 Calories; 7g Fat; 10g Protein; 48g Carbohydrate; 4g Dietary Fiber

Caesar Green Beans

Categories   Side Dishes / Vegetables

This is light vegetable dish can be served with any entrée and made within minutes. To save time, use frozen green beans and cook until almost tender.

Serves 6   Preparation Time 15 minutes
               Total Time 30 min (if using fresh green beans)

4 c	green beans, rinsed & snapped into 2 pieces
1 lg	clove garlic, minced
1 T	olive oil
2 T	red wine vinegar
3/4 c	croutons
1 T	soy parmesan cheese

Steam green beans until almost tender about 20-25 minutes.   In a small skillet over medium heat, sauté garlic in oil 1 minute. Add vinegar, beans, croutons, and cheese. Toss. Remove from heat and serve.

Per Serving: 63 Calories; 3g Fat; 2g Protein; 9g Carbohydrate; 3g Dietary Fiber

Carrot-Winter Squash Bake

Categories   Side Dishes / Vegetables

This will remind you of the traditional Thanksgiving sweet potato casserole but much more flavorful. You can also substitute yams, pumpkin, or sweet potatoes.

Serves 6   Preparation Time 20 minutes   Total Time 1 hour

1 med	winter squash
1 T	butter
4 med	carrot, grated
1 med	onion, minced
1/4 c	raisins
1/2 c	apple juice
1 t	dill, fresh, or 1/2 t. dried
2 T	maple syrup
1 t	cinnamon
1/3 c	walnuts, chopped
	salt and pepper to taste

Cut squash in half. Scoop out seeds. Place face down on cookie sheet and bake until done (30-40 min.) Cool and scoop squash from shell, mash and set aside. In a large sauce pan, melt butter and add carrots, onions, currants and sauté 3 minutes. Add apple juice and simmer 5 minutes. Add syrup and spices. Stir in squash and mix well. Cover and simmer 5 minutes. Uncover - and simmer until liquid is absorbed.

Per Serving: 140 Calories; 6g Fat; 3g Protein; 21g Carbohydrate; 3g Dietary Fiber

Cranberry Yams

Categories   Side Dishes / Vegetables

This colorful vegetable mix can be served as a holiday side dish or with any entrée. You can substitute sweet potatoes or winter squash.

Serves   12   Preparation Time 20 minutes   Total Time 1 hour

2 c	cranberries, fresh or frozen
3/4 c	orange juice
1/2 c	walnuts, chopped
1/2 c	brown sugar
1/2 t	salt
1/2 t	cinnamon
1/8 t	nutmeg
4 med	yams

Heat oven to 350. Spray 9 X 13 casserole dish. In large bowl, mix all except potatoes. Peel potatoes and slice 1/2 inch thick. Toss potatoes in mixture. Coat well. Cover and bake 40 minutes.

* To make your own brown sugar mix 1/2 C. fructose + 2 T. maple syrup.

Per Serving: 128 Calories; 3g Fat ; 2g Protein; 24g Carbohydrate; 3g Dietary Fiber

Egg Rolls with Plum Salsa

Categories   Side Dishes / Vegetables

Served with steam or fried rice, these vegetarian egg rolls can be used as main dish or a side dish. You can serve with bottled plum or sweet and sour sauce or use the Plum Salsa recipe.

Serves 20   Yields 20   Total Time 1 hour

1 pkg	egg roll wrappers
3 c	bean sprouts
3 c	cabbage, shredded
1 1/4 c	snow pea pods, fresh, chopped into 1/2 pieces
1 1/4 c	zucchini, julienne
1/2 c	green onion, chopped
1/2 c	carrot, grated
1 t	ginger
1/2 t	garlic powder
2 T	olive oil

Steam vegetable except bean sprouts for about 10 minutes (crisp tender) and drain. Add bean sprouts, seasonings and mix. Divide the vegetables among each egg roll wrapper and roll up starting with a corner and tucking in the ends. With your finger wet the edge of the last corner with water and seal.

Place seam side up on a baking sheet. With a pastry brush, lightly brush each egg roll with the olive oil. Turn each egg roll and brush the other side. Bake at 400 until lightly browned and crisp. Turn over and continue baking until lightly brown. Approximately 30 minutes. Garnish with black and white sesame seeds and drizzle salsa.

Per Serving: 31 Calories; 1g Fat; 1g Protein;
4g Carbohydrate; 1g Dietary Fiber

Garden Potato Patties

Categories   Side Dishes / Vegetables

This is a low-fat version of the fried potato patties that we are familiar with. Serve as a side dish for any entree. They are also a nice addition to breakfast.

Serves   8 (2 patties each)   Preparation Time 45 minutes

6 med	potatoes, baked or steamed, peeled
1 c	millet, cooked or any whole grain
1/2 c	flour
1/2 c	onion, diced
1/2 c	carrots, grated
1/2 c	bell pepper, diced
3 T	Bragg's amino liquids (see pantry list or substitution list)
1/2 t	oregano
1/2 t	basil
1/4 t	garlic powder
1 c	seasoned bread crumbs

In a large bowl, mash potatoes. Add flour, millet, and mix well. Sauté vegetables until tender. Add spices and Bragg's and sauté for 1 minute. Add vegetables to potatoes. Mix well and form into 16 patties. Oil a large baking sheet. Lay each patty in the bread crumbs to coat. Place on baking sheet and bake at 375 for 15 minutes. Turn and bake for another 15 minutes.

Per Serving: 261 Calories; 2g Fat; 8g Protein; 54g Carbohydrate; 5g Dietary Fiber

Herbed Vegetable Sauté

Categories   Side Dishes / Vegetables

The vegetables make a perfect side dish, but they can also be used as a filling for a burrito or pita. The fennel gives this dish a slight licorice flavor.

Serves 8   Preparation Time 25 minutes

4 c	red potato, chopped
2 T	peanut oil
1/2 c	onion, chopped
1 t	fennel seeds
1 t	thyme, 1 T. if fresh
1 t	parsley, 1 T. if fresh
1 t	basil, 1 T. if fresh
1 sm	zucchini, chopped
1 c	corn
1 T	olive oil
	salt and pepper to taste

Steam potatoes until almost tender (about 10 minutes). Drain and set aside. Heat peanut oil in large skillet and add onion and sauté 3 minutes. Add herbs and toss. Add potatoes, zucchini and corn and sauté 5 minutes. Season with salt and pepper and drizzle olive oil over potatoes.

Per Serving: 130 Calories; 5g Fat; 3g Protein; 19g Carbohydrate; 2g Dietary Fiber

Polenta

Categories   Side Dishes / Vegetables

This is a versatile gourmet meal or side dish. Use in Italian or Mexican cuisine. Top with grilled vegetables, salsa, marinara sauce, or be creative with your own ideas.

Serves 8   Preparation Time 30 minutes

2 c	corn meal
6 c	water
2 t	pizza seasoning
5 T	Bragg's amino liquids (see pantry list), or soy sauce
1 t	garlic powder
2 T	soy parmesan cheese

Bring water to a boil. Turn the heat down some. Add cornmeal and stir constantly while adding the rest of the ingredients. It will thicken. Pour into a lightly sprayed 13 X 9 baking dish. Refrigerate until cool. Then cut into desired shapes. May reheat in oven or grill on a BBQ grill.

Per Serving: 120 Calories; 2g Fat; 4g Protein; 62g Carbohydrate; 4g Dietary Fiber

Potato Vegetable Gratin

Categories   Side Dishes / Vegetables

Crispy on the top, yet soft inside, this potato casserole is an ideal side dish for any meal. It can also be used as a filling for a burrito or pita.

Serves 4   Preparation Time 15 min   Total Time 45 min

3 med	potatoes, baked until almost tender
1/2 c	onions, sliced
1/2 c	summer squash, sliced
2 T	butter, or soy margarine
2 lg	garlic clove, minced
1 t	parsley
1/2 t	paprika

Cool potatoes enough to handle. Peel if you want. Slice 1/4 thick. In a bowl mix remaining ingredients except margarine. In a 9 X 13 baking dish layer vegetables ending with potato slices on top. Divide the butter and dollop on top of potatoes. Cover and bake on 350 for 30 minutes.

Per Serving: 128 Calories; 5g Fat; 2g Protein;
19g Carbohydrate; 2g Dietary Fiber

Rice Pilaf

Categories   Side Dishes / Vegetables

The fresh taste of thyme makes this side dish complimentary to any main dish. Use any whole grains, brown rice or a combination.

Serves 8   Yields 4 cups   Preparation Time 5 minutes
                                    Total Time 1 hour

2 T	butter, or soy margarine
1/2 c	green onion
1 med	garlic clove, minced
1T	thyme, fresh, chopped
2 T	parsley
1 1/2 c	brown rice, cooked
3 c	vegetable broth, or your favorite broth
	salt and pepper to taste

Heat butter in pan, add onion, garlic, thyme, and parsley. Sauté 5 minutes. Add rice and stir until translucent, 2-3 minutes. Pour broth into rice. Heat until boiling. Reduce and simmer covered until liquid is gone (about 1 hour).

Per Serving: 132 Calories; 5g Fat; 3g Protein; 19g Carbohydrate; 2g Dietary Fiber

Roasted Potatoes

Categories   Side Dishes / Vegetables

A perfect side dish, or roll up in a tortilla for a quick burrito.
Stuff a pita and garnish with fresh salsa.

Serves 4   Preparation Time 10 min   Total Time 45 min

3 lg   potatoes, cut into 1" cubes, (or use 5-6 red
                potatoes)

Dressing

3 T   Italian salad dressing (Ranch, Parmesan, or your
              favorite oil dressing)
1 T   olive oil
1 t   parsley
1/8 t   red pepper, dried
2 lg   minced garlic

In a medium sized bowl mix the dressing till smooth. Toss
potatoes in mixture. Spread potatoes in a single layer on a
lightly sprayed cookie sheet. Bake at 400 until tender
(approximately 30 - 40 minutes turning once or twice to prevent
sticking).

Per Serving: 81 Calories; 9g Fat; trace Protein;
1g Carbohydrate; trace Dietary Fiber

Spicy Lime Corn on the Cob

Categories   Side Dishes / Vegetables

This dressing gives the corn a tangy, spicy taste. Just drizzle over the corn before serving.

Serves 4   Preparation Time 15 minutes

3 T	lime juice, fresh
2 t	olive oil
1 t	chili powder
1 t	cumin
2 T	cilantro, fresh, chopped
4 lg	ears of corn

In a large pot of boiling water, cook fresh corn for 3 – 5 minutes and drain. Mix up the rest of the ingredients and drizzle over corn.

Per Serving: 107 Calories; 4g Fat; 3g Protein; 19g Carbohydrate; 3g Dietary Fiber

Sweet Acorn Squash

Categories   Side Dishes / Vegetables

This warm and slightly sweet squash is a great side dish for any meal. You can use any winter squash or pumpkin.

Serves 4   Preparation Time 15 minutes   Total Time 1 hour

1 med	acorn squash
1/2 c	maple syrup
1 T	cinnamon

Peel off the outside layer of the squash. Cut off one of the ends, and scrape out the seeds. Slice in thin rings. Lay them on a lightly sprayed sheet pan and brush them with maple syrup and sprinkle them with cinnamon. Put them in the oven on 350 for 45 min.

Per Serving: 151 Calories; trace Fat; 1g Protein; 39g Carbohydrate; 3g Dietary Fiber

Tabbouleh No-Cook Salad

Categories   Side Dishes / Vegetables

This traditional middle-eastern dish can be made using any whole grains or a combination of each. The ingredients are the same as the Tabbouleh Salad recipe except the bulgur wheat is soaked and sprouted to make a completely raw dish.

Serves 6   Yields 3 cups   Preparation Time 20 min
                                                            Total Time 1 hour 20 min

1 c	wheat, bulgur, cracked
1 1/2 c	boiling water
1/2 c	parsley, fresh, chopped
2 T	mint, fresh, chopped
2 T	olive oil
2 T	lemon juice, fresh
1 c	tomatoes, chopped
1 med	green onion, minced
3/4 c	cucumber, peeled and chopped
2 lg	garlic cloves, minced
	salt and pepper to taste

Combine wheat and water and soak until wheat is hydrated and water is absorbed - at least 60 minutes. Add the rest of the ingredients except the tomatoes. Mix well. Add tomatoes and mix gently. Serve at room temperature or chill.

Per Serving: 159 Calories; 5g Fat; 6g Protein; 25g Carbohydrate; 5g Dietary Fiber

Tofu Wild Rice

Categories   Side Dishes / Vegetables

This dish makes a wonderful side dish or adding by a salad, it can be a hearty main dish. Use other cooked, whole grains such as Kashi, wheat, or quinoa.

Serves 8   Preparation Time 15 minutes
                 Total Time 1 hour 30 minutes

1 c	brown rice
1 c	wild rice
1/2 c	pine nuts
6 c	water
1/2 c	mushroom, sliced
1/2 c	onion, diced
1 pkg	tofu, firm, Chinese style-cubed
2 T	Bragg's amino liquids, or soy sauce
1 T	basil, fresh
1 T	thyme, fresh
1 T	parsley, fresh

Heat oven 350. Toast nuts in oven for 5 minutes. Rinse the rice. Place rice and water in 2 quart casserole dish. Lay the rest of the ingredients over the rice - do not stir. Cover and bake until water is gone - approximately 1-2 hours.

Per Serving: 228 Calories; 6g Fat; 9g Protein; 32g Carbohydrate; 3g Dietary Fiber

Vegetable Sauté

Categories   Side Dishes /Vegetables

You can use any assortment of fresh vegetables. Try adding mushrooms, seeds or nuts. Use this as a side dish or serve over rice for a main dish.

Serves 4   Preparation Time 20 minutes

1 c	broccoli, chopped
1 c	cauliflower, chopped
1 c	carrots, chopped
1 c	asparagus, chopped
3 T	Bragg's amino liquids or soy sauce
1 t	oregano
1 t	basil
1 lg	garlic cloves, minced
1/2 t	salt

Steam vegetables until slightly tender. Place Bragg's, garlic and spices in a hot pan. Add vegetables and sauté until tender.

Per Serving: 40 Calories; trace Fat; 4g Protein; 94g Carbohydrate; 3g Dietary Fiber

Salads

Strawberry and Cucumber Salad

Cole Slaw

Categories   Salads

Not only is this a colorful salad, but more flavorful than a traditional coleslaw.

Serves 8   Preparation Time 15 minutes

1 med	green cabbage, finely shredded (may us a mix of red and green)
1 med	bell pepper, finely chopped
1 med	carrot, finely chopped
1/2 c	green onion, finely chopped
3/4 c	coleslaw dressing, see recipe or use your favorite low-fat dressing

If using the Coleslaw Dressing recipe in this book, make up the dressing ahead of time and chill to blend seasonings. In a large bowl place all of the vegetables. Pour the dressing over the salad. Mix well and chill.

Per Serving: 116 Calories; 9g Fat; 1g Protein; 7g Carbohydrate; 1g Dietary Fiber

Cranberry Ring Salad

Categories   Salads

I use Emes flavored gelatin because it is plant based (see Pantry list). You can use regular Jello if you wish. This salad is a great addition to a Thanksgiving or Christmas dinner or anytime you are in the mood for cranberries.

Serves   12   Preparation Time 030

1 6-oz pkg	gelatin, raspberry, Emes brand
1/4 t	salt
1/4 t	cinnamon
2 c	boiling water
1 16-oz can	cranberry sauce, whole
2 T	grated orange peel
1 c	orange sections, diced small
1 c	apples, chopped
1/2 c	walnuts, chopped
dash	cloves

Dissolve Jello, salt, and spices in boiling water. Add cranberry sauce and rind. Mix until well blended. Chill until thickened. Fold in apples, oranges, nuts and pour into a Jello ring (6 c) and chill until firm. When ready to serve, dip the bottom of the ring in hot water to loosen and turn over on a plate. Slice into sections.

You can also use individual serving dishes. Garnish with an orange slice.

Per Serving: 111 Calories; 3g Fat; 2g Protein; 21g Carbohydrate; 1g Dietary Fiber.

Fresh Summer Squash Salad

Categories   Salads

Use yellow squash or zucchini or mix the two. Serve with fresh garlic bread and a side of rice for a complete meal.

Serves   6   Preparation Time 30 minutes

4 sm	summer squash, sliced 1/4 thick (rounds)
2 med	green onions, chopped
1 T	olive oil, for sautéing
1 med	avocado, peeled and cubed
1 4-oz can	green chili, diced
1 med	lemon, juiced
2 T	olive oil
1 med	garlic clove, minced
	salt and pepper to taste
4 c	lettuce leaves, chopped

In a skillet sauté squash in 1 T oil 4 minutes. Add garlic and green onion and sauté for 1 more minute. Place in bowl and chill for 1 hour. Add green chilies and mix. Add avocado and toss. Mix 2 T. oil, lemon juice, and salt and pepper, and drizzle over the salad. Serve over a bed of lettuce.

Per Serving: 154 Calories; 12g Fat; 3g Protein; 12g Carbohydrate; 4g Dietary Fiber

Garden Salad

Categories   Salads

Use any of your favorite dressings (see recipes) and mixed greens such as kale, spinach, chard, spring mix, or different kinds of lettuce.

Serves 4   Preparation Time 20 minutes

4 c	lettuce leaves, mixture of romaine, green or red leaf lettuces
1/2 c	beets, raw and shredded
1/2 c	carrots, shredded
1/2 c	radishes, sliced thin
1/2 c	red cabbage, chopped
1/2 c	cucumber, chopped

Rinse fresh greens with cold water and drain. Tear into bit-sized pieces and place into a large bowl. Add the rest of the ingredients. Garnish with sprouts and sunflower seeds. Pour over your favorite dressing.

Per Serving: 28 Calories; trace Fat; 1g Protein; 6g Carbohydrate; 2g Dietary Fiber

Italian Pasta Salad

Categories   Salads

This pasta salad can be served with seasoned beans and fresh whole wheat bread for a delicious meal. You can also use Italian, Caesar, or one of your favorite dressings.

Serves 8   Preparation Time 30 minutes

Dressing

1/2 c	mayonnaise, Hain's eggless or Veganaise (see Pantry list)
2 T	red wine vinegar
1 med	garlic clove, minced
1 t	basil
1/2 t	oregano
1/2 t	salt
1/4 t	pepper
	or use 1 T Italian Herb Seasoning for the herbs.

Vegetables

2 1/2 c	macaroni, whole grain (rainbows, elbows, etc), cooked (follow directions on package)
1 c	tomatoes, chopped
1/2 c	bell pepper, chopped
1/2 c	black olives, sliced
1 c	cucumbers, chopped

Blend first 7 ingredients until smooth to make dressing. Place the vegetables and the macaroni in a large bowl. Pour dressing over and mix well. Chill to blend seasonings.

Per Serving: 216 Calories; 12g Fat; 4g Protein; 23g Carbohydrate; 2g Dietary Fiber

Mandarin Peanut Salad

Categories   Salads

Adding the tofu, turns this salad into a main dish. You can omit the tofu for a lighter salad.

Serves 6   Preparation Time 30

2 T	peanut oil
1 8-oz pkg	tofu- lite, Chinese style –firm (drain off water, slice and pat dry)
8 c	lettuce leaves (Romaine, spinach or mixed greens
1/3 c	peanuts
1 8-oz can	mandarin oranges, drain, reserve juice

Sauté tofu in the peanut oil until lightly browned. Drain on paper towel. Chop the lettuce leaves and divide on 4 plates. Layer with tofu, peanuts and mandarin oranges. Pour Sesame Tahini dressing over salad. Although the recipe shows 31 grams of fat, you would not use all of the dressing because, the recipe makes a cup.

Dressing: See Sesame Tahini Dressing recipe or use prepared

Per Serving: 225 Calories; 19g Fat; 6g Protein; 12g Carbohydrate; 3g Dietary Fiber

Mandarin Spinach Salad

Categories   Salads

This salad makes a wonderful side dish or a main meal. You can substitute the spinach for fresh mixed greens, or dried chow mien noodles.

Serves 6   Preparation Time 30 minutes

1 8-oz can	mandarin oranges, drain and save liquid
1 12-oz pkg	tofu, firm, drained and cubed-Chinese Style
1 med	cucumber, julienne
1 lg	carrot, julienne
1 lg	celery, julienne
2 med	green onions, julienne
1 c	bean sprouts
4 c	spinach, chopped
2 T	peanut oil
1 T	sesame seeds

Sauté tofu in the peanut oil until light brown. Drain. Place spinach in bowl and layer the rest of the ingredients. Pour Sesame Tahini dressing over salad. Sprinkle with sesame seeds.

Dressing: Sesame Tahini Dressing (see recipe or use prepared)

Per Serving: 237 Calories; 17g Fat; 7g Protein; 17g Carbohydrate; 3g Dietary Fiber

Southwest Millet Salad with Cilantro Lime Vinaigrette

Categories   Salads

This is a great salad to accompany a Mexican meal or as a side dish for sandwiches, burritos, or wraps.

Serves 8   Preparation Time 20 minutes

1 c	millet, cooked, or any whole grain
1 1/2 c	corn, cooked
1/4 c	cilantro, chopped, fresh
1 14-oz can	black beans, rinsed and drained
1 lg	avocado, sliced
	for dressing use the Cilantro Lime Vinaigrette recipe or use you favorite light vinaigrette.

Cook millet or whole grain according to directions. Drain any left over water. Add vegetables. Pour over dressing. Add salt and pepper to taste.

Per Serving: 273 Calories; 5g Fat; 13g Protein; 46g Carbohydrate; 10g Dietary Fiber

Strawberry and Cucumber Salad

Categories   Salads

Cool and refreshing, this is a great summer or dessert type salad.

Serves 4   Preparation Time 20 minutes

2 T	mint, fresh, chopped
1 t	fructose, powdered
2 T	lite rice vinegar
1 T	strawberry jam
3 T	olive oil
2 med	cucumbers, chopped
8 oz	strawberries, quartered
1/4 c	orange and yellow bell peppers sliced thin for garnish
	black pepper to taste

In a medium bowl or layered on a plate, place cucumbers and strawberries. Sprinkle the bell peppers over the top. In a small bowl, whisk the rest of the ingredients. Pour the dressing over cucumbers and strawberries. Chill to blend flavors. Garnish with sprigs of mint or micro greens.

Per Serving: 133 Calories; 11g Fat; 1g Protein; 10g Carbohydrate; 3g Dietary Fiber

Summer Squash with Basil Vinaigrette

Categories   Salads

This delightful vegetable salad can accompany any meal. It is colorful and a great addition to a picnic.

Serves 6   Preparation Time 20 minutes

1 c	zucchini, thinly sliced
1 c	yellow squash, thinly sliced
1/2 c	red onion, thinly sliced
1/2 c	red bell pepper, thinly sliced
1/2 c	green bell pepper, thinly sliced

Steam squash for 3 minutes. Place in serving dish. Add onions and peppers. Toss with Basil Vinaigrette dressing (see recipe), a regular Vinaigrette dressing of your choice or fresh lemon juice.

Per Serving: 19 Calories; trace Fat; 1g Protein; 4g Carbohydrate; 1g Dietary Fiber

Tabbouleh Salad

Categories   Salads

*This is a traditional Middle Eastern dish. Use any whole grain
or a combination of grains such as wheat bulgar, kashi, millet,
quinoa, etc. or mix some of each. Serve warm or cold.*

Serves 8   Yields 6 cups   Preparation Time 20 minutes

3 c	brown rice, cooked (or other whole grains)
2 c	plum tomatoes, seeded and diced
1 med	cucumber, diced
2 med	green onions, diced
2 lg	garlic cloves, minced
1/4 c	mint leaves, fresh, chopped
4 T	olive oil
1/2 c	parsley, fresh chopped
4 T	lemon juice
Pinch	allspice
	salt and pepper to taste

Dressing: In small bowl mix olive oil, lemon juice, and minced
garlic.

In large bowl combine the rest of the ingredients. Pour dressing
over salad and mix well. Chill or serve warm.

*Per Serving: 163 Calories; 8g Fat; 3g Protein;
 22g Carbohydrate; 2g Dietary Fiber*

Taco Salad

Categories   Salads

This salad is a complete meal in itself. Fast and fun - the whole family will love it. Use any whole grains (Kashi, millet, quinoa, etc). Use any fresh greens (spring mix, red leaf or romaine lettuce, etc)

Serves 6   Preparation Time 20 minutes

3 c	corn chips, crushed
3 c	brown rice, cooked,
1 14- oz. can	black beans, rinsed and drained
1 14 -oz. can	seasoned chili beans (or your favorite cooked bean recipe)
1/2 c	soy cheese, grated (optional)
8 c	green leaf lettuce, chopped, or mixed greens
1 c	carrots, grated
1 c	red cabbage, grated
1 med	tomato, chopped

Mix the two beans and heat in a saucepan. Make sure the rice is hot too. On 6 plates, layer in order. Garnish with sour cream, your favorite salad dressing, salsa, or guacamole

Per Serving: 469 Calories; 9g Fat; 19g Protein; 81g Carbohydrate; 15g Dietary Fiber

Three Bean Salad

Categories   Salads

If you love the Three Bean Salads found at many famous salad bars, then you will love this recipe. You can change the taste by changing the dressing. It is very fast and easy.

Serves   12   Preparation Time 15 minutes

4 med	sun-dried tomato halves, sliced thin
1/2 c	red onion, chopped
1/4 c	vinaigrette dressing, or any oil based salad dressing you prefer
1 15-oz can	green beans, drained
1 15-oz can	kidney beans, drained
1 15-oz can	garbanzo beans, drained
2 med	garlic cloves, minced

Rehydrate tomatoes in hot water for 10 minutes and drain. Place all vegetables in a medium bowl. Toss with vinaigrette and chill to blend flavors.

Per Serving: 268 Calories; 3g Fat; 16g Protein; 47g Carbohydrate; 16g Dietary Fiber

Tomato Cucumber Salad

Categories   Salads

This cool, delicious salad is great in the summer or fall when fresh tomatoes are available. It is colorful and light, and can be served as a side dish for any entrée or sandwich.

Serves 4   Preparation Time 20 minutes

3 med	cucumber, sliced thin
4 med	Roma tomatoes, sliced thin
1/2 c	red onion, sliced thin

Place the vegetables in a medium bowl. Pour over the dressing. Chill.

Dressing

2 med	garlic cloves, minced
1/2 t	salt
2/3 c	low-fat yogurt, or tofu yogurt, or a light mayonnaise (Hain's, Veganaise)
1/8 c	olive or flax oil
1/8 c	parsley, chopped
1/8 c	mint, chopped

In a small bowl make dressing by mixing garlic, salt yogurt, parsley, mint, and olive oil.

Per Serving: 112 Calories; 5g Fat; 3g Protein; 16g Carbohydrate; 3g Dietary Fiber

Waldorf Salad

Categories   Salads

*This cool and delicious salad is perfect for any time of the year.
For a great meal, you can add sautéed tofu and grapes for a
great salad filling for a pita or placed on fresh greens.*

Serves 8   Preparation Time 20 minutes

4 med	apples, chopped
1 c	celery, chopped
1/2 c	walnuts, chopped
3 T	lemon juice

Place chopped apples in a medium bowl and pour over lemon
juice. Mix well to coat. Add nuts and celery.
Mix dressing and pour over salad. Chill for 1-2 hours. Serve
over a bed of lettuce.

Dressing

2/3 c	low-fat yogurt, or tofu yogurt, or a light mayonnaise (Hain's, Veganaise)
1 T	fructose
1/2 t	cinnamon

*Per Serving: 242 Calories; 20g Fat; 2g Protein;
16g Carbohydrate; 3g Dietary Fiber*

Sandwiches

Hummus and Veggie Rollups

BBQ Onion Avocado Sandwich

Categories   Sandwiches

Serve on a bun, whole grain bread, stuff in a pita, or wrap in a
tortilla. Garnish with lettuce or sprouts and dill pickle.

Serves 4   Preparation Time 30 minutes

1 lg	onion, white or yellow, sliced thinly
1/2 c	barbeque sauce, see BBQ sauce recipe or use your favorite
1 lg	avocado, sliced 1/3-inch thick
1/2 c	carrot, grated
1/2 c	summer squash, grated
1/2 c	red cabbage
4 med	whole wheat buns

Sauté onion in BBQ sauce until tender. May add a little water
while sautéing if needed. Lightly steam carrots, squash, and
cabbage until almost tender. Divide onion with sauce evenly on
4 buns. Divide vegetables evenly among sandwiches. Place
avocado on top. May garnish with sprouts and pickle.

Per Serving:: 244 Calories; 10g Fat; 7g Protein;
33g Carbohydrate; 6g Dietary Fiber

Eggless Salad Sandwich

Categories   Sandwiches

*Serve on bread, toast, pita or crackers, or scoop onto a bed of
fresh greens.*

Serves 6   Preparation Time 20 minutes

1 12-oz pkg	tofu, lite, firm, silken
2 T	green onion, minced
2 T	celery, diced
1 T	relish, sweet
12 pieces	whole wheat bread

Drain tofu and mash with fork to the consistency of chopped egg.
Mix onions, celery, and relish. Mix in dressing (see below).
Refrigerate until chilled.

Dressing

1/3 c	mayonnaise, Hain's eggless or Veganaise(see Pantry list)
1/4 t	turmeric
1/4 t	dry mustard
1/4 t	dill weed
1/8 t	pepper
1/8 c	seasoned rice vinegar

Blend all until smooth.

*Per Serving: 170 Calories; 3g Fat; 7g Protein;
31g Carbohydrate; 4g Dietary Fiber*

Falafel

Categories   Sandwiches

Falafel is a great meat substitute. There are many different varieties. This recipe makes a great sandwich when stuffing in pitas, placing on whole wheat buns or bread, or wrapping in tortillas.

Serves   4   Preparation Time 30

1 14-oz can	garbanzo beans
1/2 c	onion, chopped
1/4 c	parsley
2 med	garlic cloves, minced
1 T	cumin
1 t	salt
1/2 t	coriander
1/2 t	baking soda
1/4 t	cayenne
1/4 c	sesame butter/tahini (optional)

Puree all in blender or food processor until smooth, except garlic. Add garlic and pulse to blend. Place 2 T. peanut oil in skillet and heat. Scoop out falafel with a small scoop and place in oil and fry until light brown. (Or you can try to broil them to avoid the oil.) Spread a pita with a tablespoon of tahini sauce (see recipe). Place a couple of falafels in a pita (or other bread) and flatten. You can garnish with romaine lettuce, grated red cabbage or other vegetables.

Per Serving: 275 Calories; 11g Fat; 12g Protein; 34g Carbohydrate; 5g Dietary Fiber

Hummus and Veggie Rollups

Categories   Sandwiches

The rollups are ideal using tortillas, pitas, or other flatbreads.
See the "Hummus" recipe or buy prepared hummus.

Serves 4   Preparation Time 20 minutes

1 c	hummus
4 med	tortillas, whole wheat
1 sm	cucumber, sliced
1 c	red cabbage, shredded
1 med	tomato, sliced
1/2 c	mushrooms, sliced
1 c	alfalfa sprouts

Spread 1/4 c hummus on each tortilla to within 1 inch of edge.
Divide the vegetables evenly among the tortillas placing them off
center. Fold the edge of the tortilla over the vegetables. Press
down to spread the vegetables. Fold the tortilla envelope style.
Serve or refrigerate until ready.

Per Serving: 271 Calories; 9g Fat; 11g Protein;
41g Carbohydrate; 7g Dietary Fiber

Sloppy Joes

Categories   Sandwiches

This old-fashioned sloppy Joe recipe is loved by all ages. Scoop on to whole wheat buns, tortillas. or fill pita pockets.

Serves 8   Yields 4 cups   Preparation Time 20 minutes

2 c	soy crumbles, (use your favorite- Boca Recipe, Amy's or Lite Life are great brands)
1 med	onion, chopped
1 med	bell pepper, chopped
1 sm	carrot, grated
1 lg	garlic clove, minced
1 8- oz. can	tomato sauce
1/2 c	catsup
3 T	water
2 T	Bragg's amino liquids

In large sauce pan, heat water. Add onions, bell, pepper, and carrot. Cover and cook until soft - about 3-5 minutes. Add crumbles, tomato sauce, catsup, and garlic. Simmer 3- 5 minutes.

Per Serving: 113 Calories; trace Fat; 13g Protein; 31g Carbohydrate; 3g Dietary Fiber

Black Bean Veggie Burgers

Categories   Sandwiches

Making your own veggie burgers is easy and economical. Roll into balls for a great "meatless ball" recipe. Alternate ingredients each time to give variety. To make cooking easier and quicker, use pre-cooked grains or veggies you have on hand.

Serves 4   Preparation Time 20 min   Total Time 50 min

1 14-oz can	black beans, cooked, drained, and mashed (you can try other types of beans)
1 c	brown rice, cooked (or try millet, barley, quinoa, etc)
1/2 c	bread crumbs, seasoned
1/4 c	onion, grated
1/2 c	carrot, grated
1/2 c	zucchini, grated
1/2 t	salt
1 t	herbs, parsley, cardamom, garlic, etc. (for a spicy version add chili powder or cumin)
1 t	Bragg's amino liquid, or soy or tamari sauce

Mix all ingredients well and form patties or small balls. Bake at 350 for 30-40 minutes, or until browned.

Per Serving: 169 Calories; 1g Fat; 8g Protein; 32g Carbohydrate; 7g Dietary Fiber

Veggie Calzones

Categories   Sandwiches

Although this recipe is placed in the sandwich section (because you can pick it up and eat it), it also makes a great main dish served with a green salad. Use any assortment of vegetables. I use my bread machine on the dough setting to make the pizza dough. It saves me time and mess. You can also use prepared hot roll mix or pizza crust.

Serves   4   Preparation Time 30 minutes   Total Time 1 hour

3 med	tomatoes, sliced
1sm.	jar roasted red peppers, chopped
1 loaf	pizza dough, whole wheat (see Pizza Dough recipe)
1 c	pizza sauce
1 c	broccoli, chopped
1 c	spinach, cut in small pieces
3/4 c	soy cheese, mozzarella, grated (optional)
1 c	zucchini, sliced thin
1 T	olive oil
1 T	rosemary, fresh, diced

On a lightly greased pizza pan, spread 1/2 dough to edges of pan. Spread with pizza sauce leaving a 1 border. Top with vegetables. Sprinkle with cheese. Roll out other 1/2 of dough and place on top of pizza. Press edges around to seal. Brush top of pizza with oil. Cut a few slits in top. Bake 350 about 20-30 minutes or until done. Cut into 8 pieces.

Per Serving: 303 Calories; 8g Fat; 3g Protein; 51g Carbohydrate; 8g Dietary Fiber

Gazpacho

10 Bean Soup

Categories   Soups

Spicy and full of flavor, this soup makes a great meal. It is fast and easy, and you can use any assortment of beans, lentil, or peas. For a complete protein, serve with a side of rice.

Serves 8   Preparation Time 15 minutes

2 c	dried beans, assorted
1	14-oz can tomatoes
1 T	dried onion
3 T	beefless broth powder + 4 cups water - or use prepared broth
1 T	parsley, dried
1 1/2 t	chili powder
1 t	garlic powder
1 t	oregano, dried
1/2 t	salt
1/4 t	pepper

Soak beans for 8 hours and rinse. In a large pot add beans, water, tomatoes, and seasonings. Simmer 1 1/2 hours or until beans are tender. You may need to add a little more water. You can also put it all in a crock pot and cook 6-8 hours.

Per Serving:: 189 Calories; 1g Fat ; 12g Protein; 35g Carbohydrate; 14g Dietary Fiber

Baked Potato Soup

Categories   Soups

This is a delicious, thick soup just right for soup bowls. You can add more liquid if you want a thinner soup.

Serves 8   Preparation Time 30 minutes

4 lg	potatoes, baked
1/3 c	butter, or soy margarine
1/3 c	flour
1 qt	rice milk
2 c	water
1/2 c	soy cheese, grated (optional)
4 lg	green onion, diced
1/2 c	soy sour cream (optional)
	salt and pepper to taste

Melt butter in pan, add flour and stir to make a roux. Add rice milk and water and simmer until thickened. Add salt and pepper. Scoop baked potatoes out of shell and save some of the skins. Mash up the potatoes and chop some of the skins to bite-sized pieces. Add to soup and heat thoroughly. Add green onion, sour cream, and cheese and cook until all is melted and well blended. You may garnish with veggie bacon bits and soy cheese.

*You may reduce calories and making a lighter soup by omitting the soy cheese and soy sour cream.

Per Serving:: 246 Calories; 12g Fat; 6g Protein; 30g Carbohydrate; 2g Dietary Fiber

Cream of Broccoli Soup
(or Cream of Vegetable)

Categories   Soups

This recipe can be a base for many soups. For fun variations, substitute the broccoli for different vegetables such as asparagus, spinach, cauliflower, mushroom, or celery. By adjusting the amount of liquid, this soup can be used in bread soup bowls or served in regular soup bowls.

Serves 8   Preparation Time 15 minutes   Total Time 1 hour

3 T	butter, or soy margarine
1 med	onion, diced
1/2 c	celery, chopped
1 med	head broccoli, chopped
2 lg	baked potato, peeled and mashed up
1 qt	"chickenless" broth, or 1 qt. Water + 4 T. "chickenless" broth powder (see Pantry list))
8 oz	rice milk
3 T	flour
1/4 c	water
	salt and pepper to taste

In a hot pan, add 3 T water and sauté onions and celery until soft. Add the stock, broccoli and the baked potatoes. Simmer for 30 minutes or until vegetables are soft.   Make a roux out of the flour and butter, or soy margarine, and add to the soup to thicken it. Add the rice milk and puree the soup. Add salt and pepper.

Per Serving: 130 Calories; 5g Fat; 4g Protein; 20g Carbohydrate; 4g Dietary Fiber

Creamy Split Pea Soup

Categories   Soups

This soup is thick and creamy and perfect for bread bowls. Add more liquid if you would like a thinner soup.

Serves 8   Preparation Time 15 minutes   Total Time 1 hour

2 c	split peas, rinsed
4 1/2 c	water
1/2 c	celery, diced
1/2 c	carrots, diced
1/2 c	onion, diced
1 t	salt
1/4 t	pepper
2 c	rice milk, or soy milk

Cover and simmer split peas and vegetables in water about 45 minutes or until soft and starting to thicken. Stir in rice milk and add salt a pepper. Heat through.

*Use less rice milk if you want a thicker soup for soup bowls.

Per Serving: 173 Calories; 1g Fat ; 12g Protein;
31g Carbohydrate; 13g Dietary Fiber

French Onion Soup

Categories   Soups

Serve with a slice of toasted, whole wheat French bread and a fresh green salad.

Serves   8   Preparation Time 30 minutes

2 med	onions, yellow or white, sliced thin
2 T	soy margarine, or butter
6 c	broth, "beefless"-prepared or 3 T powdered broth, with 6 c. water (see pantry list)
2 T	"chickenless" broth powder (see pantry list)
1/8 c	fresh thyme, minced
	salt and pepper to taste
1 med	French bread, whole wheat

Bring the broths and minced thyme to a soft boil. Cook soy margarine and onions in a sauté pan until soft. Add onions and the salt and pepper to the broth and heat. Ladle into soup bowls. As an option you can sprinkle soy cheese on top and let stand for a few minutes until cheese melts.

Per Serving: 192 Calories; 5g Fat; 5g Protein; 32g Carbohydrate; 2g Dietary Fiber

Gazpacho

*This traditional Italian soup is usually served cold making it
great the warmer seasons, and for any time of year.*

Serves 8   Preparation Time 30 minutes

2 12-oz cans	tomatoes, diced
4 med	green onions, chopped
1	med. red bell pepper, chopped
2 med	cucumber, chopped
1 c	avocado, chopped
2 T	garlic, chopped
1/2 c	red wine vinegar
1/2 c	olive oil
1/4 c	lemon juice
dash	cayenne
1 qt	tomato juice
2 T	"chickenless" broth powder + 2 cups water, or 2 c. prepared broth
	salt and pepper to taste

Mix all ingredients and chill to blend flavors. Garnish with
cilantro and serve warm or cold.

*Per Serving: 180 Calories; 14g Fat; 3g Protein;
18g Carbohydrate; 3g Dietary Fiber*

Lari's Curried Pumpkin Soup

Categories   Soups

Given to me by my sister, Lari, this soup is great any time of the year. Try using cooked squash, yams, or sweet potatoes. Serve with fresh biscuits and a fresh garden salad.

Serves 8   Preparation Time 30 minutes

1/2 lb	mushrooms, sliced
1/2 c	onions, chopped
2 T	butter, or soy margarine
2 T	flour
1 t	curry powder
3 T	"chickenless" broth powder (see pantry list) + 3 c water
	or use prepared broth
1 15-oz can	pumpkin
1 10-oz can	coconut milk, or Rice milk equivalent to lower fat content
2 T	honey
1/2 t	salt
1/4 t	pepper
	dash nutmeg

Sauté mushrooms and onions in butter. Stir in flour and curry powder. Add broth powder and water. Mix well and cook until thickened. Add rest. Heat and serve.

Per Serving: 143 Calories; 10g Fat; 2g Protein; 13g Carbohydrate; 2g Dietary Fiber

Lari's Quick Minestrone

Categories   Soups

My sister, Lari, created this recipe from sampling a favorite Italian restaurant's soup. Yum! It is super fast and easy. Way to Go!

Serves 8   Preparation Time 30 minutes

2 8-oz cans	tomato sauce
2 c	noodles, cooked (use whole wheat elbows, corkscrew, bow ties, etc.)
3 c	water
1 16-oz can	cooked beans, white, kidney, etc., rinsed and drained
1 16-oz can	diced tomatoes, with liquid
1 c	carrot, grated
1 c	bell pepper, diced
1 c	celery, diced
3/4 c	onion, diced
2 lg	garlic cloves, minced
1 T	Italian seasoning, dried (or use 1 t each of oregano, basil, garlic)
	salt and pepper to taste

In a small amount of water, sauté the vegetables until soft. Pour all ingredients into a large pot. Simmer 5 minutes. May add water if necessary.

Per Serving: 168 Calories; 1g Fat; 8g Protein; 34g Carbohydrate; 6g Dietary Fiber

Lentil and Brown Rice Soup

Categories   Soups

This soup is loaded with flavor. Beans and brown rice make a complete protein. Serve with whole wheat hard rolls or French bread.

Serves 8   Preparation Time 15 minutes   Total Time 1 hour

4 T	beefless broth powder + 4 1/2 c. water (or use prepared broth)
3/4 c	lentils, dried
1/2 c	brown rice, uncooked
1 14-oz can	tomatoes, chopped with juice
1 med	carrot, chopped
2 stalks	celery, chopped
1/2 t	basil
1/2 t	oregano
1/2 t	thyme
1 T	parsley
1/2 t	salt
1/4 t	pepper

Mix all ingredients in a large pot. Cover and simmer 45 minutes or until lentils and rice are done.

Per Serving: 120 Calories; 1g Fat; 7g Protein; 23g Carbohydrate; 7g Dietary Fiber

Mixed Bean and Winter Squash Stew

Categories   Soups

*This hearty stew is perfect for the cooler weather. Serve with
warm bread and a fresh salad.. For a quicker version, use 1-2
16-oz can(s) cooked, unseasoned beans.*

Serves 8   Preparation Time 20   Total Time 1 hour

1 c	beans, dry, assorted
1 8-oz can	tomato sauce
1 T	olive oil
1 med	onion, chopped
1 med	bell pepper, chopped
3/4 c	corn
1 sm	zucchini, chopped
2 med	celery, chopped
3 T	vegetable broth powder + 3 cups water, or prepared broth
2 lg	garlic clove, minced
2 c	winter squash, peeled and diced
1 T	oregano
1 T	chili powder
1/2 t	cumin
	salt and pepper to taste

Soak beans over night and rinse off water. Add fresh water and
cook the beans and until soft, drain. Sauté the vegetables (except
the squash) in the oil for 5 minutes. In large pot put the 3 c.
liquid, vegetables, beans, garlic, squash, and spices. Cook for
30-45 minutes or until squash is tender

*Per Serving: 154 Calories; 3g Fat; 8g Protein;
28g Carbohydrate; 9g Dietary Fiber*

Spinach Tomato Soup

Categories   Soups

*This is a fast and easy tomato soup you can serve any time of the year. Knudsen's Very Veggie juice has less sodium than V-8. Check your health food store for other brands. *When a recipe call for apple or white grape juice, I buy the baby food juices. They are usually the right amount of juice for a recipe so you don't have to make up a large amount.*

Serves   4   Yields 4 cups   Preparation Time 15 min

1 16-oz can	tomatoes, diced
2 c	vegetable juice or tomato juice
4 T	white grape juice
1T	lime juice
1T	fructose
2 t	Worcestershire sauce
1t	salt
1t	black pepper
3 dashes	Tabasco sauce
1/2 c	spinach, fresh and chopped; if frozen, thaw and drain

Heat to boiling and serve.

Per Serving: 78 Calories; trace Fat; 2g Protein; 19g Carbohydrate; 2g Dietary Fiber

Cranberry Coffee Cake

Apple Cake with Apple Syrup

Categories   Desserts

Serve warm and topped with the Apple Syrup, with a side of applesauce, or plain

Serves   16   Preparation Time 30 minutes   Total Time 1 hour

2 c	whole wheat flour
1 T	baking powder
1 t	baking soda
1 lg	egg, or substitute (substitution list)
1/4 c	fructose
1/2 c	applesauce, or oil
3/4 c	apple juice concentrate
1/2 c	water

Mix dry ingredients and wet ingredients separately. Lightly spray an 8 X 8 pan and bake for 30-35 minutes at 350. Cool and slice and top with apple syrup.

Apple Syrup

1 1/2 c	apple juice concentrate
1 t	cinnamon
1 c	apple, grated
1/2 c	walnut, chopped
2 T	arrowroot powder, or cornstarch
4 T	water

In a small bowl, mix arrowroot and water. In a medium sauce pan, bring the rest to a boil. Add arrowroot mixture. Cook until thickened. Cool and pour over dessert.

Per Serving:: 106 Calories; 3g Fat; 3g Protein;
20g Carbohydrate; 2g Dietary Fiber.

Apple Cranberry Streusel

Categories   Desserts

This is a wonderful warm, autumn dessert. The cranberries add a slightly tart flavor. Serve as is or with a scoop of frozen Rice Dream or Soy Dream dessert.

Serves   20   Preparation Time 30 minutes   Total Time 1 hour

4 c	apples, sliced 1/4-inch thick
1 c	fresh cranberries, (raisins, or other dried fruit)
1 c	walnuts, chopped
2 T	lemon juice
1/4 c	fructose
1 t	cinnamon

Mix all ingredients and lay in a 9 X 13 lightly sprayed pan. Layer with topping and bake 350 for 40 minutes.

Topping

6 T	flour
2/3 c	quick cooking oats
4 T	fructose
1 t	cinnamon
dash	nutmeg
3 T	shortening (Spectrum, softened, or soy margarine)

Mix dry ingredients. Cut in shortening until crumbly. You can use butter if you wish but it raises the fat content somewhat.

Per Serving:: 100 Calories; 4g Fat ; 2g Protein; 16g Carbohydrate; 2g Dietary Fiber

Banana Cream Pie

Categories   Desserts

This dessert tastes rich and luscious, but it is low in fat and not too sweet. You may top with a small amount of non-dairy topping if you wish. You can also use a prepared graham cracker piecrust although it will raise the fat content.

Serves   16   Preparation Time 20 minutes

2 1/2 med	bananas
1/2 med	banana, sliced thin, keep separate
1 T	lemon juice
1/4 t	banana extract
1/4 c	oil
1/2 c	fructose
1/4 t	salt
2 c	tofu-lite, silken
1 c	Post grape nuts, or use a 9 prepared graham cracker crust.

Blend all but sliced bananas. Add sliced bananas and mix carefully. Pour grape nuts into an 8X8 pan. Carefully ladle filling over grape nuts. Chill 3 hours. When the filling is set, cut into 8 slices.

Per Serving:: 85 Calories; 4g Fat; 1g Protein; 14g Carbohydrate; 3g Dietary Fiber

Banana Oatmeal Cake

Categories   Desserts

Top this cake with Carob Topping (see recipe), serve plain, or dust lightly with powdered fructose.

Serves   20   Preparation Time 15 minutes
                            Total Time 1 hour 15 min

2 c	whole wheat flour
2 c	oats
1 t	salt
1 T	baking powder
1/2 t	baking soda
1/4 c	fructose
1 t	banana extract
5 med	bananas, mashed
2/3 c	raisins
1 lg	egg, or substitute (see substitution list)
1/4 t	nutmeg
1/2 t	cinnamon
1/4 t	allspice
2/3 c	rice milk
2/3 c	water
1 t	vanilla

Mix dry and wet ingredients separately. Then mix together. Lightly spray a 9 X 13 baking dish. Bake at 375 degrees for 45-60 minutes, or until done. Cut into 20 square pieces.

Per Serving:: 162 Calories; 2g Fat; 5g Protein; 34g Carbohydrate; 4g Dietary Fiber.

Berry Couscous Pudding

Categories   Desserts

Use fresh or frozen blueberries, raspberries, strawberries, blackberries, or a mixture. They all taste great. The couscous gives it a tapioca texture.

Serves   6   Preparation Time 15 minutes   Total Time 30 min

2 c	berries
3 c	apple juice
1/4 t	salt
1 c	couscous
1 t	grated orange peel, or lemon

Mix all. Cover and simmer 10 minutes. Turn off heat and let sit 15 minutes. Spoon into dishes. Garnish with fresh berries.

Per Serving: 182 Calories; trace Fat; 4g Protein; 40g Carbohydrate; 3g Dietary Fiber

Berry Mousse

Categories   Desserts

This dessert is a family favorite. You can use any berries or fruit such as fresh peaches or bananas. Experiment with combinations. Packed with calcium and protein, you'll never know you're eating healthy.

Serves 6   Preparation Time 15 minutes

1/2 c	apple juice
1 t	agar agar, or Emes gelatin (see substitution or pantry list)
1 pkg	tofu- lite, silken
3 c	berries, or other fruit
3 T	fructose
1 t	vanilla

In a small pan, bring apple juice to a simmer. Add agar-agar. Stir until dissolved (about 5 minutes). Blend all in a blender until smooth. Pour into 6 serving dishes. Chill at least 1 hour.

Per Serving: 68 Calories; trace Fat; trace Protein; 17g Carbohydrate; 2g Dietary Fiber

Carob Banana Pudding

Categories   Desserts

Here is a sweet, low-fat, non-dairy pudding. You can leave the carob out and have fresh banana pudding.

Serves   4   Preparation Time 15 minutes

2 c	bananas, mashed
3/4 c	tofu-lite, silken
2 T	vanilla
1 T	carob powder
1/4 c	maple syrup

Place all ingredients in a blender. Blend until smooth. Pour into 4 serving dishes. Chill for at least 2 hours to set.

Per Serving: 201 Calories; 1g Fat; 4g Protein; 44g Carbohydrate; 3g Dietary Fiber

Carob Bon Bans

Categories   Desserts

This is a sweet, but healthy treat. Try changing cereals, adding nuts, or using different sweeteners such as brown rice or maple syrup or part molasses.

Serves   10   Yields 20   Preparation Time 20 minutes

1/2 c	honey
1/4 c	peanut butter, or other nut or seed butters
2 T	carob powder
1/2 c	flax seed, ground
1 T	sesame seeds
1/4 c	sunflower seeds
3/4 c	dried fruit, chopped, typically cherry-but try a variety
1 1/2 c	puffed rice cereal
1/4 c	coconut flakes

In a medium sauce pan, mix honey and peanut butter. Bring to a boil and simmer on low for 2 minutes. Remove from heat, add carob, and mix well. Add the rest of the ingredients. Drop by teaspoon full and on lightly sprayed, piece of wax paper. Place the coconut in a bowl and roll the bon bans in the coconut to cover. Refrigerate until set.

Per Serving: 189 Calories; 9g Fat; 5g Protein; 26g Carbohydrate; 4g Dietary Fiber

Carob Chiffon Pie

Categories   Desserts

Light and delicious, this pie is a hit with chocolate lovers.

Serves   16   Preparation Time 20 minutes

1/2 c	carob powder
3/4 c	fructose
1 1/2 t	cornstarch, or substitution
	(see substitution list)
1 1/2 c	rice milk
1 lg	egg, or substitute (see substitution list)
1 1/2 t	vanilla
2 12 - oz pkgs	tofu-lite, firm, silken
1/4 c	Emes gelatin, + 1/8 c water
1 c	Post grape nuts

In a large sauce pan, mix carob, fructose, cornstarch, and egg.
Stir in rice milk. Cook over medium heat until thickens, stirring
constantly. Add vanilla and Emes mixture to stir to dissolve.
Pour into a bowl to cool, stirring constantly. Place tofu in
blender, add pudding, and blend. Spread Grape Nuts in an 8X8
pan. Carefully ladle mixture slowly over grape nuts and chill
until set, about 4 - 6 hours. Cut into 16 pieces.

Per Serving: 83 Calories; 2g Fat; 3g Protein;
15g Carbohydrate; 3g Dietary Fiber

Carob Couscous Cake

Categories   Desserts

This rich tasting dessert is for chocolate lovers. Carob, a great chocolate substitute, is high in calcium, very nutritious, and caffeine free.

Serves   12   Preparation Time 30 minutes

3/4 c	pecans, ground
2 1/2 c	water
1/2 c	fructose
1/4 c	carob
1 c	couscous
1 T	vanilla

In a medium pan, stir together water, fructose, carob, couscous. Simmer and cook until thick (5-10 minutes). Add vanilla and mix. Spread into 9" spring form pan. Sprinkle 1/4 cup pecans over cake. Pour filling over cake and sprinkle rest of pecans over top. Chill 2 hours or until set. Cut into 12 slices.

Filling

1 1/4 c	carob chips
2 1/4 c	tofu-lite, silken, at room temp.
3 T	fructose

Melt chips in pan stirring constantly. In blender, place tofu, fructose, melted chips. Blend until smooth. Add a little water if necessary.

Per Serving: 226 Calories; 8g Fat; 7g Protein; 33g Carbohydrate; 2g Dietary Fiber

Carob Tofu Brownies

Categories   Desserts

No one will believe that these brownies are good for you. Eat and enjoy!

Serves   16   Preparation Time 25 min   Total Time 50 min

1 c	tofu-lite, silken
1/2 c	white flour
1 c	whole wheat flour
3 T	white flour
1 c	water
1 c	fructose
1 1/2 T	baking powder
1 t	salt
1 t	vanilla
2/3 c	carob powder
1/3 c	oil, or substitute (see substitution list)
	Add nuts or seeds if you wish

Blend tofu, 3 T flour, and 1 cup water until smooth. In a small saucepan, pour in the tofu mixture and cook over low heat until heated (about 3 minutes). Transfer into a mixing bowl and add fructose, salt, vanilla and mix well. In a small bowl, mix carob and oil until smooth and add to tofu mixture. Stir in remaining 1 1/2 cup flour and baking powder until blended. Pour into a lightly sprayed 8X8 baking dish and bake 25-30 minutes at 350. Cool and cut into 16 squares.

Per Serving: 182 Calories; 6g Fat; 3g Protein; 32g Carbohydrate; 3g Dietary Fiber

Carrot Pineapple Cookie

Categories   Desserts

If you love soft, moist cookies, this delightful healthy cookie resembles the traditional carrot cake.

Serves 24   Yields 4 dozen   Total Time 1 hour

4 c	whole wheat flour
2 lg	eggs, or substitute (see substitution list)
1 t	baking soda
1 t	ginger
1 c	fructose
2 T	baking powder
2 t	cinnamon
1 c	applesauce
1 24-oz can	crushed pineapple
1 c	raisin
1 t	vanilla
3 c	carrot, grated

Mix dry and wet ingredients separately. Add together and mix well. Drop by spoonfuls on a lightly greased cookie sheet and press. Bake at 375 for 15 minutes.

Per Serving: 170 Calories; 1g Fat; 4g Protein; 40g Carbohydrate; 4g Dietary Fiber

Carrot-Pineapple Cake

Categories   Desserts

Serve plain, add pineapple topping, or dust with powdered fructose

Serves 20   Preparation Time 20 minutes   Total Time 1 hour

3/4 c	fructose
3/4 c	applesauce
2 lg	eggs, or substitute (see substitution list)
2 1/2 c	whole wheat flour
3/4 t	salt
1 1/4 t	cinnamon
1 1/2 T	baking powder
1/2 t	baking soda
1 - 14 oz. can	pineapple, crushed
1 t	vanilla
2 c	carrot, grated

Mix dry ingredients together in large pan. In a medium pan, mix wet ingredients. Mix in carrots and pineapple and add to dry ingredients. Lightly spray a 9 X 13 pan. Pour batter into pan. Bake at 350 for 45 min. to 1 hour until done. Cut into 20 pieces.

Topping
1 c	pineapple, crushed
1/2 c	water
1 T	arrowroot powder (or cornstarch)

Mix arrowroot powder (or cornstarch) in water until dissolved. Add to pineapple and its juice. Heat and simmer until thickened.

3 pts

Per Serving: 123 Calories; 1g Fat; 3g Protein 28g Carbohydrate; 3g Dietary Fiber

Cranberry Coffee Cake

Categories   Desserts

Try using other fruit such as blueberries, raspberries, etc

Serves   20   Total Time 1 hour

3 c	whole wheat flour
1/2 t ea	salt, ginger, cinnamon
1 T	baking powder
1 1/2 t	baking soda
1/2 c	tofu, soft
1/4 c	fructose
1 c	cranberries, fresh or frozen
2 lg	eggs, or substitute (see substitution list)
3/4 c	rice milk, + 1 T apple cider vinegar
1 2/3 c	apple juice
1/3 c	raisins

Mix dry ingredients in a large bowl. Blend well tofu, rice milk and apple juice. Add in egg or egg replacer and blend. Add mixture to dry ingredients. Fold in cranberries and raisins. Pour batter into a lightly sprayed 9X13 baking dish. Sprinkle Streusel (see below) over batter. Bake. at 350 for 30-40 minutes or until done in the center. Cool in pan. Cut into 20 pieces.

Streusel
1/3 c fructose, 3/4 c oats, 1/2 c nuts, chopped, 4 T butter, (or soy margarine)

Mix first 3 ingredients. Cut in butter/soy margarine until crumbly

Per Serving: 190 Calories; 6g Fat ; 5g Protein; 32g Carbohydrate; 4g Dietary Fiber.

Fruit Popsicles

Categories   Desserts

This is a wonderful, healthy snack, perfect for anytime of year. You can mix any fruits or juices you wish. The tofu adds creaminess to the texture along with important minerals and nutrients.

Serves 16   Preparation Time 10 minutes

1 12-oz can	fruit juice, concentrate-pineapple, orange, etc.
1 12-oz can	cold water, from juice can
1 12 oz pkg	tofu- lite, silken
1 lg	banana, or other fruit (strawberries, mangos, berries, melons, etc)

Blend all in blender and pour into 16 plastic popsicle molds. Freeze at least 8 hours. If you don't have molds you can use small paper cups with a popsicle stick. Just peal the paper off when ready to eat.

Per Serving: 16 Calories; trace Fat; 2g Protein; 2g Carbohydrate; trace Dietary Fiber

Gingerbread with orange glaze

Categories   Desserts

This dessert will surely bring back memories of your childhood. You can use the glaze, eat it plain, or dust with a little powdered fructose. The tofu adds extra calcium and protein.

Serves   16   Preparation Time 15   Total Time 45 minutes

1 2/3 c	whole wheat flour
2 t	baking powder
1 t	baking soda
1 1/2 t	ginger
3/4 t ea	salt, cinnamon
1/4 c	tofu
1/2 c ea	fructose, molasses, boiling water
2/3 c	applesauce

Preheat oven to 350. Lightly spray an 8 X 8 pan. In a medium bowl, sift flour, powder, soda, ginger, salt, and cinnamon. In a blender, puree tofu, fructose, molasses, and applesauce. Fold tofu mixture into flour. Add boiling water and mix well. Pour batter into pan and bake 25-30 minutes.

Glaze

1/2 c	fructose, powdered
2 T	orange juice

Glaze - In a small bowl, whisk together orange juice and powdered fructose. Drizzle over warm cake.

Per Serving: 150 Calories; 1g Fat; 2g Protein; 37g Carbohydrate; 3g Dietary Fiber

No-bake Pumpkin Pie

Categories   Desserts

This light pumpkin pie reminds you of chiffon. Emes gelatin is a plant based gelatin you can use in place of the animal-based Knox gelatin if you wish.

Serves   16   Preparation Time 20 minutes

1 12-oz pkg	tofu-lite, firm, silken
1 1/2 c	pumpkin, canned
2/3 c	rice milk
4 t	vanilla
2/3 c	fructose
1 t	cinnamon
1 1/4 t	pumpkin pie spice
1/8 c	Emes gelatin, + 1/2 c water
1 c	Post grape nuts, or a prepared 9" graham cracker crust or whole wheat crust

Place the first 7 ingredients in a blender and blend until smooth. Make Emes mixture - Bring water to a boil and stir in Emes until smooth. Add to blender and blend until smooth. Spread grape nuts in an 8X8 pan. Carefully ladle filling over grape nuts and chill until set. About 4-6 hours. Cut into 16 slices.

Per Serving: 89 Calories; 1g Fat; 3g Protein; 13g Carbohydrate; 3g Dietary Fiber

Oatmeal Raisin Cookies

Categories   Desserts

Oatmeal cookies are a longtime favorite. These cookies are healthy and great for breakfast or snack time.

Serves 18   Yields 3 dozen   Total Time 1 hour

1/2 c	applesauce, or oil
1/2 c	fructose
1 1/4 c	soy or rice milk
2 t	vanilla
1 lg	egg, or substitute (see substitution list)
1 1/4 c	whole wheat flour
1 t	baking powder
1 t	baking soda
1 t	salt
1 1/2 c	quick-cooking oats
1 c	raisin
1 t	cinnamon

Mix applesauce, fructose, soy milk, egg, vanilla. Beat until smooth. In a large bowl, mix dry ingredients. Add wet ingredients to dry and mix well. Drop by spoonfuls onto a lightly greased cookie sheet. Press with a fork. Bake at 350 degrees for 10 minutes, or until the sides start to turn brown.

If you replace the applesauce with Spectrum shortening, or vegetable oil, you would cream the shortening or oil together with the fructose and then add the rest of the wet ingredients.

Per Serving: 125 Calories (2 cookies); 1g Fat; 3g Protein; 27g Carbohydrate; 2g Dietary Fiber

Peanut Butter Cookies

Categories   Desserts

*Healthy and guilt free, this old fashioned recipe satisfies the
sweet tooth in all of us.*

Serves   18   Yields 3 dozen   Preparation Time 15 minutes
                                       Total Time 1 hour

1 1/2 c	peanut butter
2/3 c	fructose
1/2 c	applesauce, or oil
1 lg	egg, or substitute (see substitution list)
1/2 t	salt
1t	vanilla
1t	baking powder
1/2 t	baking soda
1 1/2 c	whole wheat flour
1/2 t	baking soda

Heat oven to 350. Mix wet and dry ingredients separately. Mix
together. Drop by spoonfuls on sheet and flatten with fork.
Bake for 10 minutes

*Per Serving: 211 Calories (2 cookies) ; 11g Fat; 7g Protein;
24g Carbohydrate; 3g Dietary Fiber*

Pineapple Cake

Categories   Desserts

You can use the pineapple topping, sprinkle with powdered fructose, or use a frosting of your choice

Serves   20   Total Time 1 hour 15 minutes

4 c	flour, 1/2 whole wheat, half white
4 t	baking powder
2 t	baking soda
1 lg	egg, or substitute (see substitution list)
1/2 c	fructose
3/4 t	salt
1 t	vanilla
3/4 c	apple sauce, or oil
1 1/2 c	pineapple juice
1 15 oz can	pineapple, crushed, in own juice
1/2 c	water

Mix dry and wet ingredients. Pour into a lightly sprayed 9 X 13 baking dish. Bake at 350 for 1 hour

Topping
1 - 15 oz can	pineapple, crushed, in own juice
1 c	pineapple juice
1/2 c	fructose
3 T	arrowroot powder, or cornstarch
1/4 c	water

In a med. saucepan mix crushed pineapple, juice and fructose. Bring to boil and thicken with the arrowroot powder and water. Cool before spooning over cake.

Per Serving: 182 Calories; 1g Fat; 3g Protein; 42g Carbohydrate; 1g Dietary Fiber

Pumpkin Bar

Categories   Desserts

This dessert/cookie is great for any occasion. You can also scoop the dough out and place on a cookie sheet for cookies. Vary by adding nuts or dried fruit.

Serves 20   Yields 20 pieces   Preparation Time 15 minutes
Total Time 1 hour

2 lg	eggs, or substitute (see substitution list0
1 - 15-oz can	pumpkin
3/4 c	fructose
3/4 c	applesauce, or oil
2 c	whole wheat flour
2 t	cinnamon
1/2 t	ginger
1/4 t	cloves
1 T	baking powder
1/2 t	baking soda
3/4 t	salt
3/4 c	raisins

Mix dry and wet ingredients separately then mix altogether. Lightly spray a 9 X 13 pan. Pour into the pan and smooth. Bake at 375 for 30-35 minutes. Check with a toothpick for doneness.

Per Serving: 119 Calories; 1g Fat; 3g Protein; 28g Carbohydrate; 2g Dietary Fiber

Pumpkin Cheesecake

Categories   Desserts

This dessert is not only perfect for Thanksgiving, but for any time of the year. It is rich in taste and low in fat.

Serves   16   Preparation Time 15 minutes
                          Total Time 1 hour

1 12-oz pkg	tofu- lite, silken, firm
1 15-oz can	pumpkin
4 oz	soy cream cheese
1/2 c	fructose
1 t	vanilla
1 T	pumpkin spice
1 c	Post grape nuts

Blend first 6 ingredients. Sprinkle Grape Nuts in an 8X8 pan. Carefully ladle over Grape Nuts or pour into prepared crust and bake for 45 minutes. Cool and chill 4 - 6 hours. Cut into 16 slices.

*Per Serving: 85 Calories; 2g Fat; 1g Protein;
11g Carbohydrate; 3g Dietary Fiber*

Barbeque Sauce

Categories   Salad Dressings / Sauces

This sauce is great on sandwiches, the Meatless Balls recipe, or as a marinade for tofu.

Serves   12   Yields 3 cups   Preparation Time 10 minutes
                                       Total Time 30 minutes

3/4 t	thyme
1/2 c	water
1/4 c	Bragg's amino liquids, or soy sauce
1/2 c	red onion
2 lg	garlic cloves, minced
1/4 t	black pepper
1/8 c	"chickenless "broth powder (see Pantry list)
1 t	mustard
1 T	liquid smoke flavoring
2 c	tomato puree
1/8 c	fructose
1/8 c	tomato paste

Sauté onions and garlic in a small amount of water until soft. Add the rest of the ingredients and bring to a boil. Reduce to a simmer, cover and cook for 20 minutes. Cool down the sauce so you can puree in a blender. Add water if needed.

Per Serving:: 38 Calories; trace Fat (0.1% calories from fat); 2g Protein; 38g Carbohydrate; 1g Dietary Fiber

Basic Pesto

Categories   Salad Dressings / Sauces

Pour over pasta, use as a garnish for dip for vegetables, add to soups, or use as a spread for sandwiches or pizza.

Serves 16   Preparation Time 15 minutes

1 c	basil, fresh
3 med	cloves garlic
1/2 c	pine nut, or walnuts
3/4 c	olive oil
1 T	lemon juice
1 c	spinach, fresh
	salt and pepper to taste

Add all ingredients in a blender and puree. Refrigerate until ready to use.

spts
Per Serving:: 169 Calories; 17g Fat; 2g Protein; 5g Carbohydrate; 3g Dietary Fiber

Basic Vinaigrette

Categories   Salad Dressings / Sauces

This is a very basic vinaigrette dressing. Add any herbs, spices, fruit or preserves to vary the flavor. Keep stored in the refrigerator until ready to use.

Serves 1 oz   Yields 3 cups   Preparation Time 5 minutes

1 c	white wine vinegar
1 t	salt
2 c	olive oil, sunflower oil, sesame oil, etc.
1 t	fructose
1 t	black pepper

Add all the ingredients in a bowl and whisk together. Store in the refrigerator until ready to use. When ready to serve whisk again. If adding preserves or fruit, place all in a blender and blend until smooth.

Per Serving:: 121 Calories; 14g Fat; trace Protein; 1g Carbohydrate; trace Dietary Fiber

Basil Spinach Pesto

Categories   Salad Dressings / Sauces

This pesto sauce can be used on pasta or as a sauce for pizza. It is also great as a spread for sandwiches or as a dip for veggies or hot bread.

Serves 6   Yields 1 cup   Preparation Time 15 minutes

3 med	cloves garlic, minced
2/3 c	pine nuts
3 c	fresh spinach
1/2 c	fresh basil
1/4 c	sun-dried tomatoes, reconstitute in hot water 10 minutes
1/4 c	water
3 T	olive oil
1 t	salt
2 T	soy parmesan cheese

Stem and wash spinach and basil. Place all except garlic, in blender. Blend until smooth. Add garlic and blend for 2 seconds. Chill to blend seasonings. Warm before using on pasta or spreading on pizza dough.

Per Serving:: 164 Calories; 15g Fat; 5g Protein; 5g Carbohydrate; 2g Dietary Fiber

Caesar Dressing

Categories   Salad Dressings / Sauces

A vegetarian version of the traditional Caesar dressing usually made with anchovies or anchovy paste. If you want a creamier dressing add a small amount of tofu mixed with a little water.

Serves 6   Preparation Time 5 minutes

2 med	garlic cloves
6 T	olive oil
4 T	lemon juice
2 t	Dijon mustard
1/2 t	salt
1/2 t	dulse —seaweed (minced)

Crush garlic and place in a bowl. Add oil and stir briskly. Discard large pieces of garlic. Add lemon juice, mustard, salt, and dulse. Mix well.   Chill to blend flavors. Shake well before serving.

Per Serving: 125 Calories; 14g Fat; trace Protein; 1g Carbohydrate; trace Dietary Fiber

Cameron's Fat-Free Vinaigrette

Categories   Salad Dressings / Sauces

This dressing is truly a hit. Serve over fresh greens or as a dipping for fruit. You can replace the raspberry vinegar with 4 oz. rice vinegar + 1 oz raspberry preserves.

Serves   12   Yields 1 pint   Preparation Time 5 minutes

4 oz	raspberry vinegar
1 T	fructose
1 t	garlic clove, minced
2 T	Worcestershire sauce
1 T	Dijon mustard
2 oz	lemon juice
8 oz	water
	salt and pepper to taste

Blend all except garlic until smooth. Add garlic and pulse until blended.   Chill to blend seasonings.

Per Serving: 11 Calories; trace Fat; trace Protein; 3g Carbohydrate; trace Dietary Fiber

Carob Sauce

Categories   Salad Dressings / Sauces

Drizzle over cakes, brownies, fresh fruit, frozen dessert, or any dessert you wish.

Serves 16   Yields 1 pint   Preparation Time 10 minutes

6 T	shortening, Spectrum, softened (see pantry and substitution lists)
1/2 c	carob powder
1 c	fructose
2/3 c	rice milk
1 t	vanilla
1/2 c	tofu-lite, firm, silken

Blend in blender. Store in refrigerator and warm slightly when serving. *You can also use butter in place of the shortening.

Per Serving: 74 Calories; .5g Fat; 1g Protein; 19g Carbohydrate; 1g Dietary Fiber

Cashew Lime Pesto

Categories   Salad Dressings / Sauces

This tangy pesto is perfect over pasta, as a pizza or sandwich spread, or drizzle over steamed vegetables.

Serves 6   Preparation Time 10 minutes

1/2 c	cashews
1 med	lime, juiced
3/4 c	basil, fresh
1 T	miso (fermented soybean paste)
1 T	olive oil
1/4 c	water, or desired consistency
1/8 t	red pepper flakes, optional
1/4 t	salt
1/8 t	pepper

Blend all until smooth.

Per Serving: 114 Calories; 8g Fat; 3g Protein; 11g Carbohydrate; 5g Dietary Fiber

Cilantro Lime Vinaigrette

Categories   Salad Dressings / Sauces

This light salad dressing has a Southwestern flair. It can be used for any fresh green, pasta, or bean salad.

Serves 12   Yields 2 cups   Preparation Time 10 minutes

1/2 c	olive oil
2 t	lime peel, grated
1/2 c	lime juice
2 T	cilantro, fresh
1/2 t	salt
2 med	garlic cloves, minced

Blend all except garlic in blender until smooth. Add garlic and pulse to blend. Chill to blend flavors.

2 pTs

Per Serving: 84 Calories; 9g Fat; trace Protein; 1g Carbohydrate; trace Dietary Fiber

Cinnamon Berry Vinaigrette

Categories   Salad Dressings / Sauces

This dressing gives a sweet and sour taste. Pour over fresh greens, or use as a marinade for tofu or vegetables.

Serves 8   Yields 3/4 cup   Preparation Time 10 minutes

1/3 c	olive oil
1/3 c	raspberry vinegar
3 T	fructose
1/2 t	salt
1/4 t	pepper
1 t	cinnamon

Wisk all the ingredients together. Chill for an hour. Wisk again before serving.

Per Serving: 106 Calories; 9g Fat; trace Protein;
8g Carbohydrate; trace Dietary Fiber

Coleslaw Dressing

Categories   Salad Dressings / Sauces

Use with the Coleslaw recipe, or for any salad dressing or dip.

Serves 8   Yields 1 cup   Preparation Time 10 minutes

1/2 c	soy sour cream
1/2 c	mayonnaise, Hain's eggless, Veganaise (see pantry list)
2 T	fructose
3/4 t	celery seed
1/4 c	water
	salt and pepper to taste

Blend until smooth. Chill to blend seasonings.

Per Serving: 148 Calories; 14g Fat; 1g Protein;
6g Carbohydrate; trace Dietary Fiber

Creamy Avocado Dressing

Categories   Salad Dressings / Sauces

This dressing is great on a taco salad, a regular salad, or over pasta. Using less water, it can be used as a dip for vegetables or crackers.

Serves 12   Yields 1 pint   Preparation Time 15 minutes

1 med	avocado, peeled and seeded
1 med	garlic clove, minced
1 c	water
2 T	olive oil
2 T	soy sour cream
1 t	dill weed
1 t	fructose
1/2 t	salt
1 T	lemon juice

Blend all except garlic until smooth. Add garlic and pulse to blend. Chill.

Per Serving: 54 Calories; 5g Fat ; trace Protein;
2g Carbohydrate; trace Dietary Fiber

Creamy Berry Vinaigrette

Categories   Salad Dressings / Sauces

This dressing gives variety as you use different berries or a combination. Try strawberries, cranberries, raspberries, blackberries, or blueberries.

Serves   12   Yields 1 pint   Preparation Time 15 minutes

1 1/2 c	berries
1 c	apple juice
1/4 c	fructose
1/3 c	olive oil
1 T	Dijon mustard
1/2 t	salt
1/2 c	tofu-lite, firm, silken

Blend all until smooth. Chill to thicken and blend seasonings.

3 pts

Per Serving: 96 Calories; 6g Fat ; 1g Protein; 10g Carbohydrate; trace Dietary Fiber

Hot Carob (Fudge) Sauce

Categories   Salad Dressings / Sauces

Use this sauce for dipping fruit as a fondue, or drizzling over frozen desserts, or cakes.

Serves 8   Yields 1 pint   Preparation Time 20 minutes

6 oz	tofu-lite, firm, silken
1/3 c	carob powder
3/4 c	rice milk, or almond milk
1/2 c	fructose
1 t	vanilla

Blend until smooth in a blender In a medium sauce pan bring to a boil. Reduce heat and simmer 10 minutes. Remove heat and pour in vanilla. It will thicken as it cools.

Per Serving: 106 Calories; trace Fat; 2g Protein; 25g Carbohydrate; 2g Dietary Fiber

Island Salsa

Categories   Salad Dressings / Sauces

Serve this salsa with chips or as a condiment. Top Polenta (see recipe or BBQ Tofu with Asparagus, etc.)

Serves 6   Preparation Time 30 minutes

2 med	tomatoes
1 med	mango
2 med	kiwi fruit
1/2 c	red bell pepper
1/2 c	yellow bell pepper
1/2 c	green bell pepper
1/4 c	green onion
2 sm	jalapeno, optional, or green chile for milder salsa
3 T	lime juice
1/4 c	cilantro, fresh
1/2 t	cumin
	salt and pepper to taste

Dice all ingredients and place in a medium bowl. In small bowl mix lime juice and seasonings and pour over vegetables. Marinate for at least one hour.

Per Serving: 66 Calories; 1g Fat; 2g Protein; 16g Carbohydrate; 3g Dietary Fiber

Peanut Dip

Categories   Salad Dressings / Sauces

For peanut butter lovers, this dip has less fat and calories but the same great peanut taste. Serve with crackers or fresh vegetables.

Serves 6   Yields 1 1/2 cups   Preparation Time 15 minutes

1 c	tofu-lite, silken, drained
4 T	chunky peanut butter
1/4 c	soy sour cream
2 T	lemon juice
1 t	Bragg's amino liquids
2 med	garlic, minced
1/4 c	green onions, diced, for garnish

Blend all except the green onions until smooth. Chill for 3-4 hours to blend seasonings. Top with green onions.

Per Serving: 101 Calories; 7g Fat; 6g Protein; 7g Carbohydrate; 1g Dietary Fiber

Plum Salsa

Categories   Salad Dressings / Sauces

This fun, unique salsa can be served with crackers or chips. It can also be used as a condiment or garnish with rice or vegetables.

Serves   6   Preparation Time 20 minutes

4 med	plums, chopped fine
1 med	mango, chopped fine
1 med	red onion, chopped fine
1-2 sm	jalapeno, diced fine
1/2 c	cilantro, fresh and chopped
1 t	salt
1/4 t	pepper

Place all ingredients in a medium bowl and mix well. Chill for 2 hours to blend flavors.

Per Serving: 60 Calories; trace Fat; 1g Protein; 15g Carbohydrate; 2g Dietary Fiber

Poppy Seed Dressing

Categories   Salad Dressings / Sauces

This dressing is great on a salad, or drizzle over raw or cooked vegetables or fresh fruit.

Serves   12   Yields 1 pint   Preparation Time 15 minutes

6 oz	tofu- lite, firm, silken
1/4 c	fructose
2 T	onion, diced
1 T	Dijon mustard
1/2 c	apple cider vinegar
1/4 c	olive oil
1 t	salt
1/2 t	paprika
2 T	poppy seeds
1/4 c	water, or as needed for consistency

Blend all until smooth and chill.

Per Serving: 79 Calories; 5g Fat; 1g Protein; 8g Carbohydrate; trace Dietary Fiber

Sesame Tahini Dressing

Categories   Salad Dressings / Sauces

Tahini is another name for sesame butter. It's about the same texture as peanut butter. This salad dressing is great on any salad, including pasta, fresh greens, and grilled tofu.

Serves 6   Yields 3/4 cup   Preparation Time 10 minutes

2 lg	garlic cloves, minced
2 T	tahini
1t	fructose, or honey
1/4 c	lemon juice
1 t	sesame seeds
1/4 t	cumin
1/4 c	vegetable oil
1/4 c	sesame oil
2 T	parsley, fresh, chopped
	salt and pepper to taste

In a blender, place all except seeds and garlic. Blend well. Add seeds and garlic and pulse to blend. Chill.

Per Serving: 202 Calories; 21g Fat; 1g Protein; 4g Carbohydrate; 1g Dietary Fiber

Spinach Dip (or Vegetable Dip)

Categories   Salad Dressings / Sauces

This dip is great for chips or fresh vegetables. You can substitute the spinach with different vegetables such as green onions, olives, bell pepper, or grated carrot to make a vegetable dip. For added color, serve in empty bell pepper shells.

Serves   12   Yields 1 2/3 cups   Preparation Time 10 minutes

1 c	tofu- lite extra-firm silken
1/4 t	salt
2 cloves	garlic, minced
2/3 c	spinach, squeeze dried
1 T	lemon juice

Blend all (except garlic) until smooth. Add garlic and blend for 2 seconds.

Per Serving: 17 Calories; 1g Fat; 2g Protein 1g Carbohydrate; trace Dietary Fiber

Sweet and Sour Sauce

Categories   Salad Dressings / Sauces

This sauce can be used as a dipping for egg rolls or grilled tofu, for Sweet and Sour Stir-fry, shish-kabobs, or as an accent to any Chinese dish.

Serves 4   Yields 1 cup   Preparation Time 15 minutes

8 oz	pineapple juice
3 T	Bragg's Liquid Amino Acid, or soy sauce
1 T	brown sugar
1 T	apple cider vinegar
2 t	cornstarch
1/2 t	ground ginger
1/2 t	garlic powder

Mix all ingredients and bring to a simmer until sauce has thickened.

Per Serving: 42 Calories; trace Fat; trace Protein; 10g Carbohydrate; trace Dietary Fiber

Tahini Sauce

Categories   Salad Dressings / Sauces

Tahini is another name for sesame seed butter. It can be found in any health food store or grocery stores containing a health food section. A great spread for sandwiches or as a dip for vegetables. Thin it with water and pour over rice and steamed vegetables. It makes a great dressing for coleslaw.

Serves   12   Yields 1 1/8 cup   Preparation Time 10 minutes

1/2 c	tahini
1/2 c	soy sour cream
1/8 c	lemon juice
	add water enough to thin to the consistency of catsup

Blend all until smooth.

Per Serving: 77 Calories; 7g Fat; 2g Protein; 3g Carbohydrate; 1g Dietary Fiber

Tofu Mayonnaise

Categories   Salad Dressings / Sauces

Use as a dip, over pasta, in potato salad, on sandwiches, or in any recipe calling for mayonnaise.

Serves   12   Yields 1 cup   Preparation Time 10 minutes

6 oz	tofu-lite, silken, firm
2 T	lemon juice
2 T	olive oil
1/2 t	salt
1 T	dill weed
1 T	Dijon mustard
1 med	garlic clove, minced

Blend all except garlic until smooth. Add garlic and pulse until blended. Chill to blend flavors and to thicken.

Per Serving: 28 Calories; 2g Fat; 1g Protein; 1g Carbohydrate; trace Dietary Fiber

Tofu Sour Cream

Categories   Salad Dressings / Sauces

Use this recipe for any recipe calling for sour cream. It is a great non-dairy substitute. Try different herbs or salad dressing to vary the flavor.

Serves 8   Yields 1 cup   Preparation Time 10 minutes

1 c	tofu-lite, medium to firm
1 t	dill
2 T	Italian dressing, or other vinaigrette

Blend until smooth. Chill to blend seasonings.

Per Serving: 13 Calories; trace Fat; 2g Protein; trace Carbohydrate; trace Dietary Fiber

Tomato Catsup

Categories   Salad Dressings / Sauces

To avoid all of the extra sugar, salt, and preservatives found in store bought catsup, you can make your own quickly and easily for about 1/2 the cost.

Serves 24   Yields 3 cups   Preparation Time 5 minutes

2	8-oz cans	tomato sauce
1	6-oz cans	tomato paste
5 T		fructose
3 T		apple cider vinegar
1/2 t		cloves
1/2 t		garlic powder
1/2 t		onion powder

Wisk all ingredients in a medium bowl until smooth. Chill to blend flavors.

Per Serving: 26 Calories; trace Fat; 1g Protein; 7g Carbohydrate; 1g Dietary Fiber

Vegetable Re'moulade

Categories   Salad Dressings / Sauces

This is a cold sauce you can drizzle over steamed, grilled, or cooked vegetables, or use for dipping as for artichokes or cold vegetables.

Serves 12   Yields 1 1/2 cups   Time 15 minutes

1 c	tofu-lite, silken
2 T	lemon juice
2 T	cider vinegar
2 T	olive oil
2 T	flax seed oil
1 t	Dijon mustard
1 t	tarragon
1/2 t	salt
1/8 t	pepper
1/4 c	green onion
1 T	capers
1 T	parsley, fresh
2 med	cloves of garlic, minced

Blend all except garlic until smooth. Add water as needed to bake the consistency of creamy salad dressing. Add garlic and blend 2 seconds. Chill to blend seasonings

Per Serving: 53 Calories; 5g Fat; 2g Protein; 1g Carbohydrate; trace Dietary Fiber

Zesty Marinara Sauce

Categories   Salad Dressings / Sauces

Serve over cooked, whole grain noodles, or use as a sauce for
Eggplant Parmesan, Baked Potato Parmesan, Pizza, or Meatless
Balls

Serves 6   Preparation Time 20 minutes   Total Time 1 hr.

3 T	"chickenless" broth powder (see Pantry list)
2 T	cloves garlic
1 med	yellow onion
1 c	carrots
1 28-oz can	diced tomatoes
2 8-oz cans	tomato sauce
3 T	parsley
2 T	basil
1 t	red pepper flakes, optional
2 T	soy parmesan cheese
	salt and pepper to taste

Sauté garlic and onions in small amount of water in medium
sauce pan. Add the rest of the ingredients except basil and
simmer for 35 minutes.   Add water if needed. Cool down, add
basil and puree in blender.

2 pts
Per Serving: 59 Calories; 1g Fat; 2g Protein;
18g Carbohydrate; 3g Dietary Fiber

Apple Butter

Categories   Miscellaneous

This is a great spread for sandwiches, crackers, breakfast breads, pancakes, French toast, etc.

Serves   12   Yields   3 cups   Preparation Time 30 minutes

2 c	apples
2 c	apple cider, or apple juice
2 1/2 T	lemon juice
1 t	cinnamon
1/4 t	clove
dash	nutmeg
pinch	salt

Peel and cut apples. Add all juices. Cook over low heat until desired thickness. Stir often to break up pieces. Add spices and salt and mix well. Heat through. Put in a jar and store in refrigerator.

Per Serving:: 32 Calories; trace Fat; trace Protein; 8g Carbohydrate; 1g Dietary Fiber

Cinnamon Applesauce

Categories   Miscellaneous

This makes a great side dish, dessert, or baby food.

Serves 12   Preparation Time 15 minutes   Total Time 1 hour

6 med	apples
1/2 c	apple cider
1 c	apple juice
1 c	fructose
1 T	cinnamon
1/8 t	nutmeg
1/4 c	apple cider vinegar
1/4 c	rice milk, or soy mild

Pour the liquid, except the rice milk, into a saucepan. Dissolve the fructose in liquid and bring to a simmer. Peel and core the apples and dice them into medium chunks. Add to the simmering liquid. Simmer until apples are soft and most of the liquid is gone- about 45 min. Add the rice milk and seasonings, and stir slowly. Chill 3 hrs.

Per Serving: 143 Calories; trace Fat ; trace Protein; 38g Carbohydrate; 2g Dietary Fiber

Flax Egg Replacer

Categories   Miscellaneous

You can use this egg replacer in recipes where eggs are called for in baking. See the Substitution List for more egg replacement ideas. Flax adds extra fiber, EFA's, and nutrients to your recipe.

Yields 3 cups   Preparation Time 10

1/2 c   flax seeds
2 c   water

Blend flax seeds to a powder. Add the water and blend until smooth. Refrigerate. 1/4 c. = 1 egg.

Fruit Juice Jelly / Syrup

Categories   Miscellaneous

This recipe is perfect for anyone who loves jelly or fruit syrup, but does not want the added sugar or artificial sweeteners of store bought brands. Use different juices or try mixing them. It's fast and easy.

Serves 12   Yields 1 1/2 cups   Preparation Time 15 minutes

1 12-oz can	apple juice concentrate, (or grape, cranberry, raspberry etc) for jelly or use 1 quart juice for syrup
1 T	Emes gelatin, unflavored (see pantry or substitution list)
1 T	arrowroot powder, or cornstarch

Mix all in a saucepan. Cook over medium heat stirring often until mixture comes to a boil. Pour into containers and refrigerated at least 4 hours

Per Serving: 49 Calories; trace Fat; trace Protein;
12g Carbohydrate; trace Dietary Fiber

Fruit Syrup - No Cook Freezer

Categories   Miscellaneous

Use any fresh fruit you like. Fresh fruit retains more nutrients and enzymes. Depending upon the fruit, preparation time varies.

Serves 40   Yields 10 cups   Preparation Time 1 hour

6 c	fruit, fresh (peaches, apricots, berries, concord grapes, etc)
1 pkg	Surejell lite, fruit pectin, or other fruit pectin
2 c	fructose
1 1/2 c	water
2 T	lemon juice, (for fruit that darkens)

Follow the no-cook freezer jam on the box of Surejell or fruit pectin. Pour into containers or Ziploc bags to freeze. Thaw before using and store in refrigerator.

Per Serving: 109 Calories; 0g Fat; trace Protein; 15g Carbohydrate; trace Dietary Fiber

193